At Issue

What Is the Role of
Technology in Education?

DISCARD

Other Books in the At Issue Series:

At Issue

What Is the Role of Technology in Education?

Judeen Bartos, Book Editor

GREENHAVEN PRESS
A part of Gale, Cengage Learning

GALE
CENGAGE Learning·

Detroit • New York • San Francisco • New Haven, Conn • Waterville, Maine • London

Elizabeth Des Chenes, *Director, Publishing Solutions*

© 2013 Greenhaven Press, a part of Gale, Cengage Learning.

Gale and Greenhaven Press are registered trademarks used herein under license.

For more information, contact:
Greenhaven Press
27500 Drake Rd.
Farmington Hills, MI 48331-3535
Or you can visit our Internet site at gale.cengage.com

For product information and technology assistance, contact us at

Gale Customer Support, 1-800-877-4253
For permission to use material from this text or product, submit all requests online at www.cengage.com/permissions.

Further permissions questions can be e-mailed to permissionrequest@cengage.com.

Articles in Greenhaven Press anthologies are often edited for length to meet page requirements. In addition, original titles of these works are changed to clearly present the main thesis and to explicitly indicate the author's opinion. Every effort is made to ensure that Greenhaven Press accurately reflects the original intent of the authors. Every effort has been made to trace the owners of copyrighted material.

Cover photograph © Todd Davidson/Illustration Works/Corbis.

LIBRARY OF CONGRESS CATALOGING-IN-PUBLICATION DATA

What is the role of technology in education? / Judeen Bartos, book editor.
    p. cm. -- (At issue)
    Summary: "What Is the Role of Technology in Education?: Books in this anthology series focus a wide range of viewpoints onto a single controversial issue, providing in-depth discussions by leading advocates, a quick grounding in the issues, and a challenge to critical thinking skills"-- Provided by publisher.
    Includes bibliographical references and index.
    ISBN 978-0-7377-6217-4 (hardback) -- ISBN 978-0-7377-6218-1 (paperback)
    1. Educational technology--Juvenile literature. I. Bartos, Judeen.
    LB1028.3.W435 2012
    371.33--dc23
                                          2012022609

Printed in the United States of America
2 3 4 5 6   17 16 15 14 13

Contents

Introduction

The potential to fundamentally change the world of education through technology has grown dramatically over the last twenty years. The emphasis on hardware of the past has been replaced with an approach focused more on quality of learning than the means of delivery. Lower costs and increased accessibility are leading the charge, as the use of technology has grown to be an equalizer—providing unprecedented innovative solutions to increase learning.

Nowhere is this more evident than in the area of assistive technology. Assistive technology is defined as any item that can be used to improve the functional capabilities of individuals with disabilities. With their portability and affordable applications, the recent introduction of various tablet computers and smartphones provide students with disabilities with an abundance of new options. Struggling readers can adjust font sizes, listen to audio books, and experience a book with an ease not possible before these products. Students with Asperger's Syndrome can download an application that helps them understand the nuances of social interactions with their peers. The touch screen proves ideal for students who have difficulty manipulating a mouse and keyboard. And given the relatively young age of these products, the possibilities for future uses appear limitless.

The explosion of online course options is another example of a true game-changing leap forward in education. At all levels, students are taking control of their own education, pursuing a level of learning not previously accessible or affordable for many. In 2001, the prestigious Massachusetts Institute of Technology (MIT) started to make select courses available for free online. Other university powerhouses such as the University of California at Berkeley, Yale University, and Stanford

University soon followed suit, leading to a vast array of free coursework taught by some of the finest instructors in the world of higher education.

But perhaps the biggest splash in free access to online instruction belongs to the Khan Academy, a nonprofit launched in 2006 by Salman Khan. Khan started out tutoring his cousin remotely, creating instructional videos online, and soon friends and other family members became interested. From this grew a library of three thousand instructional videos viewed by over one-hundred million learners throughout the world. Khan Academy is committed to keeping its product free and available to anyone.

Critics argue that online learning cannot and should not replace interactions with teachers and other students in a classroom. But *Wired* magazine writer Clive Thompson points out in his July 2011 article 'How Khan Academy Is Changing the Rules of Education,' that educators are taking advantage of this tool and integrating Khan coursework into their existing curriculum. Teachers that have expressed frustration in the past about having to "teach to the middle," trying to teach a group of students the same material at the same pace, now have the ability to reach kids at all levels, Thompson says. In addition, online learning tools such as Khan Academy free up teachers to focus on higher level instruction for their students.

The School of One is another promising program that seeks to change the education equation. "Reimagining the classroom to meet the needs of every child" is the goal of the School of One. This innovative pilot for teaching middle school was developed by the New York City Department of Education. Using technology and computer algorithms, the school generates individualized learning plans, combining work on computers with small group and lecture style instruction to accommodate the unique learning style of each student. Arthur E. Levine, president of the Woodrow Wilson National Fellowship Foundation, describes the School of One concept: "The School of One turns the current model of education on its head, flipping the relationship between teaching and learning. Student learning becomes the focus—the driver—of schooling," Levine says.

But for all the promise of advances in technology for leveling the playing field and improving outcomes there are children who are in danger of being left out. "Economically disadvantaged children face tremendous challenges in accessing technology, and these challenges could affect school readiness and achievement as one group of children comes to school each day with superior technology skills and an ever-growing knowledge base, while the other group lags behind," says Donna Celano and Susan B. Neuman in a November 2010 article in *Educational Leadership*.

Students with computers and other technology at home have built-in advantages that poorer children do not enjoy. Even the best of afterschool programs or library systems cannot replace the easy access that technology at home provides. If the potential of technology is to be truly realized, inequities among socioeconomic groups must be recognized and alleviated.

Despite the obstacles and difficulties schools may encounter when grappling with how to effectively use technology, the rewards seem to outweigh the costs. The future quality of education will depend on the creativity and innovative ability of educators and students to raise the level of achievement using all tools and talents at their disposal.

British author, educator, and creativity expert Ken Robinson sums it up in his book, *The Element—How Finding Your Passion Changes Everything*. "The fact is that given the challenges we face, education doesn't need to be reformed—it needs to be transformed. The key to this transformation is not to standardize education, but to personalize it, to build achievement on discovering the individual talents of each child, to put students in an environment where they want to learn and where they can naturally discover their true passions." The viewpoints in *At Issue: What Is the Role of Technology in Education?* reflect this and other perspectives on this important topic.

1

Technology Alone Cannot Reform Education

Rick Hess

Rick Hess is a resident scholar and director of educational policy studies at the American Enterprise Institute for Public Policy Research. Hess is the author of The Same Thing Over and Over: How School Reformers Get Stuck in Yesterday's Ideas. *His writing has also appeared in the* New York Times, Washington Post, *and* U.S. News & World Report.

Millions of dollars have been poured into American schools to purchase more technology with less than impressive results. Most student usage of technology does not involve higher order thinking. It does involve a lot of cutting and pasting and using the computer as an encyclopedia—activities that aren't very innovative. Focusing on the tools for educational reform rather than education itself is an expensive exercise in futility.

I'm sure my friends at the Department of Education were thrilled to read in the Raleigh-based *News & Observer* that North Carolina school districts are using their Race to the Top [RTT] funds to advance structural reform by ... purchasing iPads. Durham, N.C. is spending $3.5 million in RTT funds to "put Apple iPads in the hands of students and teachers at two low-performing schools." Durham Public Schools Superintendent Eric Becoats said, "Our kids are telling us, 'This is how we learn. This is what we want.'"

Ah-ha, yes, this is the change we've been waiting for. Look, I own an iPad. I like the iPad. But I'll tell you, when I've been to schools that feature one-to-one computing, personal computers, and iPads, they seem to get mostly used in one of two ways. Neither impresses me. The first involves students working on graphics, clip art, powerpoints, or adding sound and visual effects to video shorts. The second is students Googling their way to Wikipedia for material to cut-and-paste into powerpoints or word files.

This was all brought home to me again, just the other week, when I had a chance to spend a couple days visiting acclaimed "technology-infused" high schools. Yet, most of what I saw the technology being used for was either content-lite or amounted to students using Google-cum-Wikipedia as a latter day *World Book Encyclopedia*. Making powerpoints and video shorts is nice, but it's only us "digital tourists" who think it reflects impressive learning.

I'm a huge fan of using technology to rethink schooling. But it's the rethinking that matters, not the technology.

Once Difficult Computer Skills Can Now Be Performed with Ease

Twenty years ago, even rudimentary video editing was technically challenging and required real skill. Today, technology makes most of this stuff a snap. It's the same reason video games like *Halo* or *Madden '11* can seem enormously challenging or complex to an adult but instinctive to a kid. It's not a question of deep knowledge so much as a learned set of routines. Unfortunately, it's easy for adults to get so distracted by the visuals, stylings, and sound that we fail to note that the content is vapid or mostly consists of Wikipedia-supplied factoids.

This is when terms like "digital natives" get dangerous. Hell, I remember my own long-ago days in high school, when we could manage the tricky feat of talking on the phone for hours while playing Atari. Yet, happily, nobody mistook these happy pursuits for learning or thought we had mastered new, invaluable skills. A student in Durham using an iPad to Google her way to Wikipedia to find a description of the Harlem Renaissance is learning no more than did a student twenty-five years ago who used an encyclopedia to find the same information (though, the fact that it's now easy to cut-and-paste rather than hand-copy the information can make it even easier for a student to avoid absorbing new knowledge).

Enthusiasts will dismiss such skepticism by touting the rich multi-media resources, the tangential link chasing, the engaging visuals, and so on. Me? I'm far from sold. If you're unsure, go visit some of these classrooms and decide for yourself.

I'm a huge fan of using technology to rethink schooling. But it's the rethinking that matters, not the technology. What matters is how we use these tools to solve problems smarter, deliver knowledge, support students, reimagine instruction, refashion cost structures, and challenge students in new ways. Unfortunately, in far too many places, educators, industry shills, and technology enthusiasts seem to imagine that the technology itself will be a difference-maker. Good luck with that.

2

Online Learning Programs Are Changing the Way Students Learn

Jason Orgill and Douglas Hervey

Jason Orgill is a fellow at the Forum for Growth and Innovation at the Harvard Business School. Douglas Hervey is a research associate at Harvard who is writing a book, along with Professor Clayton Christensen, on aligning incentives in health care.

Online education has grown substantially in American schools in recent years. Advances in technology have allowed online learning programs to innovate in ways that were not possible in the past. As online learning becomes more individualized, more students are able to reach their full potential. Fears that teachers would be replaced have been largely unfounded as the most effective models use a blended approach that includes face time with teachers and downloadable lessons and exercises through an online component.

Four years ago Harvard Business School Professor Clayton Christensen predicted that online education would take off slowly and then hit everyone by surprise: the S-curve effect. And indeed, while it initially grew slowly, online education has exploded over the past several years. According to the 2010 Sloan Survey of Online Learning, approximately 5.6 million students took at least one web-based class during the fall 2009 semester, which marked a 21% growth from the previous year.

As for K-12 learning, more than 3 million students took an online course in 2009. That's up from 45,000 in 2000. Experts predict that online education could reach 14 million in 2014.

Consider a recent *Economist* article (September 2011) featuring Bill Gates's educational poster child: Khan Academy, founded by Salman Khan in 2006. Khan's business model is simple, yet impactful. As the *Economist* noted, it flips education on its head. Rather than filling the day with lectures and requiring students to complete exercises after school, Khan focuses on classroom exercises throughout the day and allows students to download more lectures after school. When students arrive at their Silicon Valley [California] suburb classroom with their white MacBooks, they begin their day doing various online learning exercises. The teacher, aware of what her students are working on based on her own monitor screen, then approaches students and provides one-on-one feedback and mentoring, tailoring her message to students' particular learning paces and needs.

> *Teachers can serve as professional coaches and content architects to help students progress in ways that they never could under most current models.*

But Khan goes beyond the computer and customized feedback. It emphasizes critical thinking and idea creation, where real learning occurs, and downplays rote lecture learning. Active problem solving makes learning much more fun and engaging for students. As the *Economist* notes, students at institutions like Khan can huddle together and solve math problems around their laptops as if they were trading baseball cards or marbles.

Despite Its Promise, Online Education Has Its Critics

Of course not everyone has warmly embraced the online education movement, namely teachers' unions. But the union's concern—that teachers will become less relevant—is misplaced. First, online education isn't the one and only teaching tool. The Sloan study indicated that the best teaching often occurs under a blended model of online learning coupled with real face time. So there will always be a need for teachers. Second, online education integration will help teachers make a more impactful influence on students. In fact, Gates, Khan, and teachers at the academy argue that online education can liberate teachers, allowing them to engage in more creative and influential one-on-one mentoring.

Other concerns relate to education quality. But integrating an online and lecture approach can actually result in students getting a higher quality education. Education Department [US Department of Education] data from last year [2010] reported that "Students in online conditions performed modestly better, on average, than those learning the same material through traditional face-to-face instruction." A blended approach combines the socialization opportunities the classroom provides with the enhanced active learning features that online learning offers. This is why former Governors Jim Hunt (North Carolina Democrat) and Jeb Bush (Florida Republican) are travelling around the country encouraging school districts to take advantage of online learning tools.

What American students most need are the tools and skills that will help them compete for the increasingly sophisticated jobs of tomorrow.

Students Have More Choices Through Online Education

Part of the challenge with revamping America's educational system resides in well-intentioned people who have focused on answering the wrong question. Nothing matters if we find the right answer to the wrong question. As Clayton Christensen and Michael Horn argued in *Disrupting Class*, insufficient money, the teachers' unions, and large classroom size, all relevant issues, are not the root cause of our schools' troubles. The real problem lies in the effects standardized education has had on a student's internal and external motivation. As the authors point out, "When education is well aligned with one's stronger intelligences, aptitudes, or styles, understanding can come more easily and with greater enthusiasm." And as the Khan Academy has demonstrated, teachers can serve as professional coaches and content architects to help students progress in ways that they never could under most current models. Students display much more enthusiasm when they can self-direct their learning paths.

A greater selection in course offerings will also motivate students and improve their educational experience. Many school districts in small, rural, and urban markets that do not have access to the breath of education available in more resource plenty areas will pull humanities, arts, economics, Chinese, and quality A.P. [advanced placement] courses into their offerings to satisfy students' unmet needs. We predict the online education movement will advance the same way that disruptive innovators have succeeded: by serving markets that are too costly or impossible for the incumbents to pursue, and then gradually moving "up-market." Targeting non-consumers creates less backlash from teachers' unions and administrators, and could even generate student referrals from incumbents themselves.

As we move into the 21st century, what American students most need are the tools and skills that will help them compete for the increasingly sophisticated jobs of tomorrow. Only then can we maximize the rising generation's potential, providing the talent necessary to keep America prosperous and competitive in the years to come.

3

Low-Income Children Lack Digital Resources

Donna Celano and Susan B. Neuman

Donna Celano is an assistant professor of communication at La Salle University in Philadelphia, Pennsylvania. Susan B. Neuman is a professor in educational studies at the University of Michigan in Ann Arbor.

Low-income children lack consistent access to high quality technology when compared to their middle-income peers. This 'digital divide' among the classes remains persistent despite the increased availability of lower priced devices and a tremendous jump in school spending on technology. The gap occurs mostly in student access outside of school, where middle-class students have computers and easy Internet access in their homes. Low-income children more often must rely on public resources such as libraries or after-school programs. But these resources can be unreliable—restrictive timeframes, high demand, and funding problems all add up to erratic availability of technology in these settings. The guidance of a parent or other adult is far different from home use as well, where time is less constrained and the atmosphere more relaxed. Over time, limitations in technology resources add up, further widening the achievement gap between the haves and have nots.

Mention the best way for educators to prepare children for the future, and the conversation will nearly always come around to technology. As blogs light up with lively con-

Donna Celano and Susan B. Neuman, "Roadblocks on the Information Highway," *Educational Leadership*, November 2010. © 2010 by ASCD. Reprinted with permission. Learn more about ASCD at www.ascd.org.

versations about iPads, netbooks, and smart phones, it's easy to forget one major roadblock to preparing all children for the future: the digital divide.

Economically disadvantaged children face tremendous challenges in accessing technology.

Most middle-class children have home computers and can access the Internet. Not so for many children from low-income neighborhoods. This unequal access has serious implications for the growing chasm between low- and middle-income students. As a Pew Foundation report found, many children are using out-of-school time to refine their technology skills. This is fine for children from middle-class homes with a home computer, but what about the millions of children who are not from such homes?

Data from the 2000 U.S. Census reveal that half of children coming from homes with annual family incomes of $75,000 or above owned home computers, but just 15 percent of those with incomes between $20,000 and $25,000 did. Internet connectivity is also an issue. Overall, 65 percent of all Americans have broadband connections in their homes. Among those Americans who make less than $25,000, 65 percent *lack* broadband access.

If low-income children want to use a computer for a research assignment or merely to wander around on the Internet, they often must rely on the public library, after-school programs, or community organizations. This safety net, however, is full of holes. Economically disadvantaged children face tremendous challenges in accessing technology, and these challenges could affect school readiness and achievement as one group of children comes to school each day with superior technology skills and an ever-growing knowledge base, while the other group lags behind.

Computer Access Strikingly Different for Low-Income and Middle-Class Children

To understand the problem, let's look at two 5th grade girls from different Philadelphia schools. Olivia, a spunky 11-year-old with tight, curly hair, lives with her parents and two brothers on a tree-lined street of neat, older homes. The computer and Internet are big parts of Olivia's life. If she forgets her math homework, she goes to a website to print out the problems or e-mails her teacher for help. During the past year, she worked on a variety of school projects using her home computer: She developed a brochure for a science project, she researched the life of a French explorer, and she looked at footage from a webcam on the school roof to check the weather.

When not working on school projects, Olivia is free to search the Internet. She has a few favorite websites, and she has been noodling around with applications such as Skype. Because she must share the computer with her two brothers, school-related projects get top priority, so she cannot spend much time on "fun" things. Still the computer is there, sitting in a converted sun porch right off the kitchen. Among Olivia and her two brothers, it is in constant use most nights and weekends.

We found strong signs that the digital divide is far from closed.

A few miles away, we find Tina, a soft-spoken 11-year-old with braids. Tina's neighborhood is a series of row homes, some inhabited, some abandoned, surrounded by poverty, high crime rates, and violence. We met up with Tina at the Salvation Army afterschool program she attends.

The computer is not nearly as big a part of Tina's life as it is Olivia's. Tina's teacher assigns little more than a worksheet or two for homework each night. It's hard, after all, to expect the many students in Tina's class without access to a home computer to complete research assignments for homework. Tina has a computer at home, but it is currently broken, and even when working it only has dial-up access. She spends about 10 hours a week here at the Salvation Army, where she sometimes uses one of six computers available to students in her after-school program. She must, however, share with the 30 to 75 other children who attend each day. In addition, the computers are housed in an office far from the main program rooms, and they are kept locked up to prevent vandalism.

When Tina does get online, she likes to play a few games— Fun Math for Kids or Study Island, two programs designed to enrich her school experience—but she isn't free to roam the Internet as she would like. First, there are the filters, which prevent her from exploring inappropriate websites but also make it hard to navigate. There is also the time issue: She can use computers only when teachers are present and usually for only about 30 minutes.

Libraries offer an enormous service to the community, providing computers, Internet access, books, and other informational materials.

We have spent a great deal of time in Tina's world, exploring the availability of technology resources as part of a case study of an urban neighborhood in North Philadelphia, where poverty rates hover at around 65 percent. We have visited or phoned all the public libraries, recreation centers, after-school programs, and community organizations in the neighborhood that might offer technology access to students after school. We found strong signs that the digital divide is far from closed.

Public Computer Access Can Include a Long Wait

Tina's after-school program at the Salvation Army is actually one of the luckier ones. Many programs serving children outside school do not have any computers. For the 7,700 children ages 5–18 in this community, we counted 128 computers in 12 programs. That comes down to .017 computers for each child.

A substantial number of those computers—23—were housed in the two local library branches. Libraries offer an enormous service to the community, providing computers, Internet access, books, and other informational materials. Without the local libraries, the computer access rate would go down to .014 computers for each child. A child visiting the library, however, faces tremendous challenges. First, he or she must vie with the increasing number of adults seeking computer access. Waits of three hours are not uncommon. Then, time limits are often set at 30 minutes, barely enough time to research or write a school report.

Computers are a precious commodity, after all, and the fear of theft is real.

One day in a branch of the Free Library of Philadelphia we found Angelica, a 7th grader, sitting on a bench watching the clock. She has a folder and a notebook on her lap; her legs swing back and forth as she silently waits for her 5:30 computer time. She is here to do research on the Internet for a Black History Month assignment due in a few days. Angelica has a computer at home, but it was stricken with a virus and has been out of commission for several months. When she arrived at the library today, the only computer time was 5:30; with the branch closing at 6:00, she has little time to work.

Because Angelica has limited computer experience, she has trouble typing. She eventually finds an article about Mary Macleod Bethune. She also needs a picture of Bethune, but she needs help figuring out how to find one. With five minutes to go, she tries to print, but there is no paper in the printer. "The library is closing in five minutes," the security guard booms over the intercom. Angelica sighs, resigning herself to coming back tomorrow and starting the process all over again.

It is worth noting that four of the five organizations with no computer access are after-school programs in local elementary schools. Each school has a computer lab, but children in after-school programs are denied access. Gloria, the director of one program, says, "I have 5th and 6th graders who want to do research projects, but they can't use the computers here at the school," she says. "I need to send them to the local library instead. It's a dangerous walk, and it would be so much better if we had computers here."

Available Equipment Is Often Outdated or Broken

For children enrolled in after-school or other programs, computer availability increases marginally, from .01 to .12 computers per child. Availability, however, does not always translate into computer use. As we saw at the Salvation Army, computers are often locked away, preventing access. Computers are a precious commodity, after all, and the fear of theft is real.

More than theft, however, is the question of upkeep. Our visit to Taller Puertoriqueño, a community organization devoted to promoting Puerto Rican culture, illustrates the difficulty. Housed in a typical corner row house emblazoned with colorful mosaics and murals depicting Puerto Rican culture, Taller Puertoriqueño offers an array of services to the community, including art, dance, and theater programs; after-school and summer camps; and teen graphic design courses.

Sandra, the program director, showed us two areas where computers are available for children's use. The first room, housed off the "homework club" area of the after-school program, is a cozy room with four relatively up-to-date computers and monitors. The children may use the computers only if they have a homework assignment requiring research or on Fridays during a free-choice period. "But," Sandra says, "we need to be careful. Someone needs to sit in here and supervise them." With no Internet filters, some children "download things they should not download. Then we get viruses and have problems."

In many after-school programs, computer use is sporadic, dictated less by children's needs and more by the organization's limited resources.

With enrollment ranging from 20 to 75 students, it's often difficult to get one of the two or three teachers to sit in the computer room. It's much easier to do an art project or run a dance class that will involve all the children. In addition, the organization has little money for technical support or new equipment.

In the adjacent art room, teens are working on graphic design projects on one of two computers. Here we find Anna, age 15, assisted by Bob, the youth program leader. They are trying to incorporate a picture into Anna's graphic arts project but aren't making much progress. Sandra shakes her head sadly. "We don't have money to upgrade these computers so students can do their projects properly. That computer was fine two years ago, but now it doesn't have enough memory. We also have printers, but they break, or we can't afford the cartridges."

In many after-school programs, computer use is sporadic, dictated less by children's needs and more by the organization's limited resources. Computers are not like books. Certainly, books may become out-of-date or break down from wear and tear. For the most part, though, books are durable. Not so with computers: They get viruses and stop working. They become obsolete relatively quickly. Printers need expensive cartridges. Technical support is hard to come by and expensive.

Of course, students could continue to access information through books, as in the past, but this will not help them develop the technological savvy they will need in the future.

Interest Is High Despite Limited Opportunities

Although computer access is noticeably lacking in this community, what is clearly abundant is interest. This was evident at Education Works, a community organization offering after-school programs in elementary schools, day-care facilities, and job-training programs. Upstairs in the program's main building, housed in a converted factory on a busy corner, is a classroom containing six relatively new computers, all in good working order and easily accessible. Because this program is housed in the organization's main building, the site has on-site technical support staff to keep the computers running smoothly. "If I have a problem with a computer or printer," says Karen, the bubbly afterschool director, "I just call Ed. He'll come right up and fix it."

Students report that teachers often will not assign projects requiring Internet access if many students do not have home computers.

The 20 students here in the middle school classrooms may use a computer once their homework is complete. If they have an assignment requiring research, they may get on earlier. Today, all homework has been finished; one teen is checking out sneakers on a retail website, another is playing a game, and another is watching a movie trailer. Every seat is taken, and other students are waiting patiently for their turn. Even though computers are accessible, the children who attend Education Works still lag in opportunities that middle-income children experience daily. Only about 35 percent of the students here have Internet access at home; the others must get their computer access at Education Works or fight for a seat at the local library.

Even when computer access is equal, its use is different in different communities. Middle-income children start using computers at a younger age and get more adult assistance. Economically disadvantaged children tend to use computer time more for entertainment than do their middle-class peers, who use it more for information gathering. Over time, the differences accumulate, meaning that middle-class children will zoom ahead and low-income children will be left behind. What started as a gap will grow into a chasm.

Teachers also use computers differently in high-poverty areas. They don't e-mail students or use course or teacher web pages as much. Students are less likely to use class time to prepare written text or create multimedia presentations on the computer. In *The Digital Disconnect*, a Pew Foundation study, students report that teachers often will not assign projects requiring Internet access if many students do not have home computers. Students with limited technology resources miss out on opportunities to use the Internet as a virtual tutor or study group, as a guidance counselor, or as a notebook to store notes and resources for future reference.

Schools Must Close the Gap for Students Without Home Access

Schools in low-income neighborhoods must help their students keep up with their more advantaged peers. Quite simply, low-income children need greater access to technology in school to make up for their limited access at home. Schools could, for example, allow access to school computer labs during evenings, weekends, and summers so that students could complete assignments or simply gain more experience exploring technology.

More important than simply offering access, though, schools need to provide low-income children with more opportunities to use technology to its fullest capacity. This includes focusing less on using computers to practice basic skills and more on teaching students strategic ways to use the computer. Many information websites, for example, will introduce students to interactive features they do not find in books and conventional print. The hyperlinks may encourage readers to navigate their own nonlinear paths through the information. Readers need to understand the advantages and disadvantages of following certain links and to discern one type of link from another. We need to integrate computers into classroom instruction as well as content-driven work.

In addition, we need to focus efforts on creating more complex in-school assignments that encourage students to use computers more effectively. Teachers can invite readers to co-author online texts as they navigate various paths through information. Or students can use digital tools to interact with others and gain access to different perspectives. Finally, schools need to collaborate more closely with local libraries and after-school programs to ensure that computers are used efficiently to complete homework and other research assignments.

The first step, though, is recognizing that the digital divide still exists. Left unchecked, it will merely keep growing. Without equal access to technology, a large number of children face the future with little hope of keeping up in today's increasingly complex world.

4

New Online Instruction Models Redefine Class Time

Bill Tucker

Bill Tucker is managing director at the Education Sector, an independent think tank that challenges conventional thinking in education policy. In his policy work for Education Sector, he focuses on technology and innovation—specifically virtual schooling, assessments, and data systems.

Instructors are using the power of technology to "flip" their lessons. Students use after school time to view lectures and demonstrations online before class, allowing instructors to use valuable class time for more advanced concepts and to explore topics much more deeply than would normally be feasible. Developing online lessons can be challenging for instructors, but the results are often more clear and concise than a real time lesson in class, and can be replayed as often as a student may need to grasp a concept. The benefits of a "flipped" classroom model appear to be many for both students and teachers, and have the potential to profoundly change the future educational landscape.

Four years ago, in the shadow of Colorado's Pike's Peak, veteran Woodland Park High School chemistry teachers Jonathan Bergmann and Aaron Sams stumbled onto an idea. Struggling to find the time to reteach lessons for absent students, they plunked down $50, bought software that allowed them to record and annotate lessons, and posted them online.

Absent students appreciated the opportunity to see what they missed. But, surprisingly, so did students who hadn't missed class. They, too, used the online material, mostly to review and reinforce classroom lessons. And, soon, Bergmann and Sams realized they had the opportunity to radically rethink how they used class time.

Bergmann notes that he now spends more time with struggling students, who no longer give up on homework, but work through challenging problems in class.

It's called "the flipped classroom." While there is no one model, the core idea is to flip the common instructional approach: With teacher-created videos and interactive lessons, instruction that used to occur in class is now accessed at home, in advance of class. Class becomes the place to work through problems, advance concepts, and engage in collaborative learning. Most importantly, all aspects of instruction can be rethought to best maximize the scarcest learning resource—time.

Flipped classroom teachers almost universally agree that it's not the instructional videos on their own, but how they are integrated into an overall approach, that makes the difference. In his classes, Bergmann says, students can't just "watch the video and be done with it." He checks their notes and requires each student to come to class with a question. And, while he says it takes a little while for students to get used to the system, as the year progresses he sees them asking better questions and thinking more deeply about the content. After flipping his classroom, Bergmann says he can more easily query individual students, probe for misconceptions around scientific concepts, and clear up incorrect notions.

Counterintuitively, Bergmann says the most important benefits of the video lessons are profoundly human: "I now have time to work individually with students. I talk to every student in every classroom every day." Traditional classroom interactions are also flipped. Typically, the most outgoing and engaged students ask questions, while struggling students may act out. Bergmann notes that he now spends more time with struggling students, who no longer give up on homework, but work through challenging problems in class. Advanced students have more freedom to learn independently. And, while high school students still occasionally lapse on homework assignments, Bergmann credits the new arrangement with fostering better relationships, greater student engagement, and higher levels of motivation.

The Flipped Classroom Concept Travels to Other Classrooms

Once Bergmann's and Sams's lessons were posted online, it wasn't long before other students and teachers across the country were using the lessons, and making their own. Across the country in Washington, D.C., Andrea Smith, a 6th-grade math teacher at E. L. Haynes, a high-performing public charter school, shares Bergmann's enthusiasm, but focuses on a different aspect of the flipped classroom. Smith, who has taught for more than a decade in both D.C.'s public charter and traditional district schools, immediately saw the benefit for students, but says she was most captivated by the opportunity to elevate teaching practice and the profession as a whole. As Smith explains, crafting a great four- to six-minute video lesson poses a tremendous instructional challenge: how to explain a concept in a clear, concise, bite-sized chunk. Creating her own videos forces her to pay attention to the details and nuances of instruction—the pace, the examples used, the visual representation, and the development of aligned assessment practices. In a video lesson on dividing fractions, for example, Smith is careful not to just teach the procedure—multiply by the inverse—but also to represent the important underlying conceptual ideas. Like Bergmann, she makes it clear that the videos are just one component of instruction. She's keen on the equivalent of a motion picture's "director's cut," where a video creator might explain the reasoning behind the examples chosen and how she would extend those activities into class time.

There is . . . some danger that the flipped classroom could be seen as another front in a false battle between teachers and technology.

"Flipping" is rapidly moving into the mainstream. Bergmann and Sams have completed a book, are in high demand across the country at educator conferences, and even host their own "Flipped Class Conference" to train teachers. The chief academic officer at Smith's school, Eric Westendorf, is taking the tools he has piloted at the school and building them into a platform for teachers everywhere to create and share videos. Most notable, though, is the emergence of the Khan Academy, an online repository of thousands of instructional videos that has been touted by Bill Gates and featured prominently in the national media.

Given education's long history of fascination with new instructional approaches that are later abandoned, there's a real danger that flipping, a seemingly simple idea that is profound in practice, may be reduced into the latest educational fad. And, in today's highly polarized political environment, it also runs the risk of being falsely pigeonholed into one of education's many false dichotomies, such as the age-old pedagogical debate between content knowledge and skills acquisition.

Flipping Is a Simple Concept That Could Have a Big Impact

But the ideas behind flipping are not brand new. For over a decade, led by the National Center for Academic Transformation (NCAT), dozens of colleges have successfully experimented with similar ideas across math, science, English, and many other disciplines. NCAT's increasingly impressive body of practice shows that thoughtful course redesigns lead to improved learning. Carol Twigg, NCAT's president and CEO, says there is no magic: course redesign is "a hard job." She's not assuming students love homework. But redesign offers an opportunity to reengage students and improve their motivation, while setting proper expectations and monitoring to "push school to the top of the list." And while many course redesigns focus on incorporating more project-based learning opportunities, Twigg's experience leads her to quickly dismiss pedagogical extremes: "If you don't have basic math skills, you can't do an interesting physics project."

There is also some danger that the flipped classroom could be seen as another front in a false battle between teachers and technology. Yet Bergmann and Sams emphasize that the "only magic bullet is the recruiting, training, and supporting of quality teachers." And while Khan Academy's prominence engenders fear of standardization and deprofessionalization among some critics, Bergmann, Sams, and Smith see instructional videos as powerful tools for teachers to create content, share resources, and improve practice. Smith admits that if such tools were available when she first started out, she "would have run to this every week when planning."

It seems almost certain that instructional videos, interactive simulations, and yet-to-be-dreamed-up online tools will continue to multiply. But who will control these tools and whether they will fulfill their potential remains to be seen. As Scott McLeod, one of the nation's leading thinkers on educational technology and the director of the UCEA [University Council for Educational Administration] Center for the Advanced Study of Technology Leadership in Education, observes, the "reason Sal Khan is so visible right now is that nobody did this instead. It would have been great if the National

Council of Teachers of Mathematics had been doing this, but someone from the outside had to fill the vacuum." His guidance to educators: "Start making!"

5

Virtual Schools May Not Provide Educational Value

Lyndsey Layton and Emma Brown

Lyndsey Layton is a national staff reporter at The Washington Post. *Emma Brown is also a reporter for the* Post *covering Virginia schools.*

Despite the growth in popularity and number of virtual schools, research on their effectiveness is scarce. Virtual education began as a flexible means to deliver instruction to a small number of students who were not served well in a traditional school setting. But it has grown to encompass a fast growing population of students, including dropouts, high achievers, and many other subsets of learners. Critics are concerned that the companies providing virtual learning are not held accountable for either the public funding they are paid nor for the achievement of students in their schools. They point out that students as young as five years old are attending virtual schools, and are missing out on vital socialization skills they will need to function in society after graduation. New regulation and oversight is needed but does not appear likely. Virtual education corporations have influenced politicians through lobbying and campaign funding, arguing that less regulation allows this emerging field to innovate and experiment.

A Virginia company leading a national movement to replace classrooms with computers—in which children as young as 5 can learn at home at taxpayer expense—is facing a backlash from critics who are questioning its funding, quality and oversight.

K12 Inc. of Herndon has become the country's largest provider of full-time public virtual schools, upending the traditional American notion that learning occurs in a schoolhouse where students share the experience. In K12's virtual schools, learning is largely solitary, with lessons delivered online to a child who progresses at her own pace.

Conceived as a way to teach a small segment of the homeschooled and others who need flexible schooling, virtual education has evolved into an alternative to traditional public schools for an increasingly wide range of students—high achievers, strugglers, dropouts, teenage parents and victims of bullying among them.

"For many kids, the local school doesn't work," said Ronald J. Packard, chief executive and founder of K12. "And now, technology allows us to give that child a choice. It's about educational liberty."

How ... do you pay for a school that floats in cyberspace when education funding formulas are rooted in the geography of property taxes?

Packard and other education entrepreneurs say they are harnessing technology to deliver quality education to any child, regardless of Zip code.

It's an appealing proposition, and one that has attracted support in state legislatures, including Virginia's. But in one of the most hard-fought quarters of public policy, a rising chorus of critics argues that full-time virtual learning doesn't effectively educate children.

"Kindergarten kids learning in front of a monitor—that's just wrong," said Maryelen Calderwood, an elected school committee member in Greenfield, Mass., who unsuccessfully tried to stop K12 from contracting with her community to create New England's first virtual public school last year. "It's absolutely astounding how people can accept this so easily."

People on both sides agree that the structure providing public education is not designed to handle virtual schools. How, for example, do you pay for a school that floats in cyberspace when education funding formulas are rooted in the geography of property taxes? How do you oversee the quality of a virtual education?

Politicians Support Increased Choice That Virtual Schools Offer

"There's a total mismatch," said Chester E. Finn Jr., president of the Thomas B. Fordham Institute, a conservative think tank, who served on K12's board of directors until 2007. "We've got a 19th-century edifice trying to house a 21st-century system."

Despite questions, full-time virtual schools are proliferating.

In the past two years, more than a dozen states have passed laws and removed obstacles to encourage virtual schools. And providers of virtual education have been making their case in statehouses around the country.

K12 has hired lobbyists from Boise [Idaho] to Boston [Massachusetts] and backed political candidates who support school choice in general and virtual education in particular. From 2004 to 2010, K12 gave about $500,000 in direct contributions to state politicians across the country, with three-quarters going to Republicans, according to the National Institute on Money in State Politics.

"We understand the politics of education pretty well," Packard told investors recently.

K12's push into New England illustrates its skill. In 2009, the company began exploring the potential for opening a virtual school in Massachusetts in partnership with the rural Greenfield school district.

But Massachusetts education officials halted the plan, saying Greenfield had no legal authority to create a statewide school. So Greenfield and K12 turned to legislators, with the company spending about $200,000 on Beacon Hill lobbyists.

About 250,000 students are enrolled in full-time public virtual schools in 30 states.

State Rep. Martha "Marty" Walz, a Boston Democrat, wrote legislation that allowed Greenfield to open the Massachusetts Virtual Academy in 2010. She acknowledged that the language was imperfect and didn't address issues of funding or oversight but said she couldn't wait to craft a comprehensive plan.

"You do what you need to do sometimes to get the ball rolling," said Walz, who accepted at least $2,600 in campaign contributions from K12, its executives or its lobbyists since 2008, according to the National Institute on Money in State Politics.

That scenario is repeating nationwide as K12 and its allies seek to expand virtual education.

About 250,000 students are enrolled in full-time public virtual schools in 30 states, according to Susan Patrick of the International Association for K-12 Online Learning, a trade association. Although that's just a fraction of the country's 50 million schoolchildren, the numbers are growing fast, Patrick said.

K12 teaches about two out of every five students in full-time online schools. Its next largest competitor is Baltimore-based Connections Education, which was recently acquired by

Pearson, the mammoth British textbook publisher. The rest of the industry consists of smaller operators and some nonprofit virtual schools.

Virtual Schools Are a Highly Profitable Business

If it were a school district, K12 would rank among the 30 largest of the nation's 1,500 districts. The company, which began in two states a decade ago, now teaches about 95,000 students in virtual schools in 29 states and the District of Columbia.

And it plans to grow. "We are now that much closer to our manifest destiny of making a K12 Inc. education available to every child," Packard said in a call with Wall Street analysts this month [November 2011].

It's a promising business. In the past fiscal year, K12 had revenue of $522 million—a 36 percent increase from the prior year, according to securities filings. Its net income after a series of acquisitions was $12.8 million. Packard earned $2.6 million in total compensation.

Packard, 48, took a roundabout route to education. A former Goldman Sachs banker, he was working as a consultant with McKinsey and Co. when he got a call from Michael Milken, the financier who pleaded guilty to securities fraud in 1990 and later became a philanthropist partly focused on education.

Packard joined Milken's education investment holding firm and ran one of his companies, a chain of preschools. About the same time, Packard was trying to find an online math course for his 6-year-old daughter. Frustrated by the dearth of options, he saw a business opportunity.

He founded K12 in 2000 with a $10 million investment from Milken and Larry Ellison, the chief executive of Oracle Corp., maker of software and hardware systems. William J. Bennett, education secretary under President Ronald Reagan, became the company's chairman, bringing his conservative bona fides and political connections to a company that originally aimed for the home-schooling market. Bennett resigned from K12 in 2005.

In the early years, Bror Saxberg served as the chief architect of K12's curriculum. With a medical degree from Harvard and a doctorate in electrical engineering and computer science from MIT [Massachusetts Institute of Technology], he was excited by the potential to transform education by applying what cognitive scientists have learned about how brains work.

"There was a terrific opportunity to finally apply some of this learning science work at scale, to make learning environments that could really make a difference for students," Saxberg said. He left the company to join Kaplan Inc. in 2009.

K12's core business—and the one proving most controversial—is full-time virtual public schools.

Kaplan is a for-profit education provider owned by The Washington Post Co. It competed directly with K12 until May [2011], when K12 acquired Kaplan's virtual-schools business. Kaplan continues to offer test-preparation courses, and in November the two companies announced an agreement to share distribution of some products and services.

K12 sells a variety of ways to learn online, ranging from hybrid schools—in which students meet in a classroom but take courses via computer—to a la carte courses purchased by traditional schools.

Last year, K12 formed a joint venture with Middlebury College to offer foreign language courses. This year, it bought a stake in a Chinese company that teaches English online.

But K12's core business—and the one proving most controversial—is full-time virtual public schools.

Students Are Enthusiastic About Their Virtual Education

For Tyler Hirata, going to school used to mean waking up at 6 a.m. and clambering aboard a yellow bus. Now he snoozes until midmorning and pads downstairs to the computer in his Dumfries [Virginia] home.

"This is fantastic!" said Tyler, 8, who had attended a Prince William County school but was enrolled this fall in the Virginia Virtual Academy—a public institution run by K12 and open to any student in the commonwealth.

Tyler said the best thing about taking third grade online is that it requires less than three hours a day. His mother is more excited that, for the first time, Tyler is reading fluently on his own.

[Teachers in virtual schools] work from home, aren't likely to be unionized and earn as much as 35 percent less than their counterparts in regular schools.

"The K12 program is phenomenal," said Michele Hirata, adding that Tyler blossomed with her daily one-on-one attention. Virtual school has been equally positive for her fifth-grade daughter, Gennifer, 10, a fast learner who spends five hours a day practicing gymnastics, she said.

Virtual class sizes tend to be larger than at traditional schools—the Virginia academy averages 60 students per teacher, according to a school document. So in the primary grades, the model relies on the intensive work of a parent "learning coach," who provides most lessons away from the computer, using books and 90 pounds of other educational materials shipped to families by K12.

In the older grades, the bulk of learning is online, with software that sometimes aims to mimic real-life experiences for students, such as a high school biology lab featuring an animated frog dissection.

Teachers monitor student progress, grade work and answer questions by e-mail or phone. They work from home, aren't likely to be unionized and earn as much as 35 percent less than their counterparts in regular schools, according to interviews with former K12 teachers.

Teachers also look for ways to help students socialize. Bethany Scanlon, a former special education teacher for K12's Ohio Virtual Academy, shipped hot chocolate and popcorn to her students one winter holiday season. They all settled in with their computers to watch "A Charlie Brown Christmas" streamed over the Internet.

"When you're teaching online, you have to be very creative," she said.

In Dumfries, Tyler said he misses some of the best parts of school, such as lunchtime. And recess. And friends.

"Believe me," he said, "if you are home-schooled, you will want friends."

During recent deliberations over virtual schooling in Virginia, a member of the state Board of Education raised the issue of socialization.

On measures widely used to judge all public schools, such as state test scores and graduation rates, virtual schools— often run as charter schools—tend to perform worse than their brick-and-mortar counterparts.

"This would appear to make it possible to go from kindergarten through eighth grade without ever stepping into a real classroom," David M. Foster said. "I'm not sure I want to encourage that. . . . Collaborative problem solving, socialization, working with other people is key not just to the global economy but to getting along in life."

41

Performance Has Been Mixed at Many Virtual Schools

While virtual schools continue to expand, their effectiveness is unclear.

"We have no real evidence one way or another," said Tom Loveless, a Brookings Institution scholar who served as a paid consultant to K12 in its early years.

A 2009 analysis by the U.S. Education Department found that there wasn't enough research to draw conclusions about how elementary and secondary students fare in full-time virtual schools compared with classrooms.

[In 2010,] about one-third of K12-managed schools met the achievement goals required under the federal No Child Left Behind law.

On measures widely used to judge all public schools, such as state test scores and graduation rates, virtual schools—often run as charter schools—tend to perform worse than their brick-and-mortar counterparts.

At the Colorado Virtual Academy, which is managed by K12 and has more than 5,000 students, the on-time graduation rate was 12 percent in 2010, compared with 72 percent statewide.

That same year, K12's Ohio Virtual Academy—whose enrollment tops 9,000—had a 30 percent on-time graduation rate, compared with a state average of 78 percent.

Last year, about one-third of K12-managed schools met the achievement goals required under the federal No Child Left Behind law, according to Gary Miron, a Western Michigan University professor who called that performance "poor."

K12 officials say the weak test results are related to the program often attracting students who struggled in regular schools.

One of K12's oldest and biggest schools is the Agora Cyber Charter, a statewide virtual school that began in Pennsylvania in 2005. The company manages the school under a contract with its nonprofit board of trustees. Enrollment this fall topped 8,000 students.

Agora has never met federally defined achievement goals.

The school markets itself as an option for at-risk students who are failing at their neighborhood school. Last year, about two-thirds of its students were low-income.

Many lived in unstable homes, said Aimee Saunders, who taught history at K12's Pennsylvania schools for four years until 2009.

Some of those children didn't have an adult who could serve as the learning coach. Instead, they were left home alone and did little or no schoolwork, she said.

Many traditional public schools have failed to help the neediest children.

"You take students who normally would struggle because of their home environment and then you put them in their home to learn," Saunders said. "It doesn't work that well."

Rapid student turnover can compound the problem. Of the 8,700 students who enrolled in 2010–11, more than a quarter withdrew during the year, according to school records.

"New students were always coming in," Saunders said, which "made it difficult to be able to focus on the students I already had."

Company officials said internal data show that Agora students—and K12 students in general—are learning at a faster rate than the national norm, even if they can't pass a grade-level test. And the longer students stay with K12, the better they perform, the company said.

But Pennsylvania has its own measure of how fast students are learning, and it showed "significant evidence" that Agora did not meet growth standards last year.

In June 2010, the state threatened to revoke Agora's charter unless the school made changes, including aligning the curriculum with state standards and expanding remediation programs for struggling students. It also insisted on more transparency so it would be clear how much K12 was receiving for different services.

Agora officials said they addressed those concerns by opening a face-to-face tutoring center in Philadelphia, for example, and hiring staff to conduct home visits.

Saunders, the former Agora teacher, says virtual schools provide an important new option for families and should be forgiven for missteps.

After all, many traditional public schools have failed to help the neediest children.

"A lot of schools are making mistakes by not trying anything different than they've tried before," she said.

Cost to Taxpayers Raises Questions of Fairness

Even some supporters of virtual schools question whether online operators are charging taxpayers fairly.

"They have no business trying to charge as much as the brick-and-mortar schools, at least over time," said Finn, of the Fordham Institute, which has commissioned a study of the cost of online schools. "Once you've got the stuff that you're going to use for fourth-grade math, for instance, you don't really need to do much with it. And it should be cheaper."

Online education companies say they are no different from textbook publishers and other businesses that profit from sales to schools.

But payments for a year's worth of online schooling can vary wildly. For instance, K12 received $3,728 per full-time student in 2009–10 for its virtual school based in Broward County, Fla., but $5,000 per student in Greenfield, Mass. K12 is getting $6,200 for each student in its D.C. school, which enrolls about 100 students.

In Pennsylvania, because of a complicated funding mechanism, K12's Agora Cyber Charter receives $6,000 to $16,000 per student for an identical course load, depending on where that student lives.

The Virginia school offers a lesson in how K12 relied on political savvy and statehouse connections to build its business.

"We don't have a real handle on what the real cost is for a virtual school," said Mitchell D. Chester, commissioner of elementary and secondary education in Massachusetts.

Jeff Kwitowski, K12's vice president for public relations, said it's "impossible" to pinpoint the true cost of educating a child in any environment, whether virtual or face-to-face. Prices vary because some schools purchase different K12 services, he said.

Funding Per Student Is Not Equitable

The Virginia Virtual Academy, another K12 venture, began enrolling full-time students across the commonwealth in fall 2009, more than a year before state law addressed this new kind of education.

The Virginia school offers a lesson in how K12 relied on political savvy and statehouse connections to build its business.

The Virginia venture was a partnership between the traditional schools of Carroll County—a rural county bordering North Carolina—and K12. Children who enrolled in the Virtual Virginia Academy were counted as Carroll County students no matter where they lived.

That was no accident.

State aid varies by school district and follows a formula based on poverty, among other factors. Affluent Fairfax County receives $2,716 per pupil from Richmond [capital of Virginia], whereas relatively poor Carroll County receives $5,421, according to the state Education Department.

This year, 66 Fairfax students are enrolled in the virtual school. Richmond is paying the virtual school twice as much for those students as it would if they attended neighborhood schools in their own county.

"Clearly, it's not a logical or equitable system," said state Sen. George L. Barker (D-Fairfax). "It's a horrible deal for taxpayers."

Barker has twice tried to change funding so that subsidies are based on where students live. Twice he was rebuffed by Gov. Robert F. McDonnell (R), a champion of school choice who successfully promoted legislation to authorize full-time virtual schools in 2010.

K12 was the only private company present during talks to craft that legislation. McDonnell has received $55,000 in campaign contributions from K12 or its executives since 2009, including a $15,000 payment to his political action committee this month [November 2011].

McDonnell was on a trade-related trip to India late last week and unavailable to comment. But his spokesman, Jeff Caldwell, said K12's political support had not influenced decisions regarding virtual schools.

"They're a corporation that is making donations to several folks," Caldwell said. "The fact that they gave some to the governor certainly did not sway his opinion."

The governor recognizes that the state needs a better way to fund virtual schools but does not want to make abrupt changes that would harm the new schools, his staff said.

McDonnell "came into office really wanting to provide options and innovation to Virginia schoolchildren," state Education Secretary Laura Fornash said. "Virtual schools [were] a major part of that."

This year, K12 opened a second virtual school in Virginia, signing a contract with Buena Vista City, near Lynchburg, where the per-pupil state subsidy is $5,850. The two schools combined have an enrollment of 540 students.

While K12 executives see unlimited horizons for online education, traditional schools are struggling with severe budget cuts.

In Carroll County, the Virginia Virtual Academy provides a revenue stream for the public school system, which collects a $500 registration fee for each out-of-district student. On top of that, the county collects a management fee—6.5 percent of the taxpayer dollars that flow to K12.

In what may be an unintended irony, Carroll County is using that windfall—$178,450 last year—to buy old-fashioned but much-needed textbooks for its brick-and-mortar schools.

6

E-texts Provide Competition for Textbook Publishers

Byron W. Brown

Byron W. Brown is a professor of economics at Michigan State University. His position includes university-wide duties helping faculty use instructional technology effectively.

Computer giant Apple is poised to revolutionize the e-text industry. With the introduction of its product called iBooks Author, it has taken on mainstream textbook publishers who have up until now held a monopoly on the market while doing little to advance e-text technology. The publishers seem content with the status quo and reluctant to innovate on design or price, leaving their e-text selections less desirable than their print counterparts. But iBooks Author is a major leap forward, providing affordable technology that gives everyone the chance to create and publish multimedia texts. An open-content world may serve to inspire the type of innovation and creativity that will propel the e-learning experience to a higher level to the benefit of students and instructors alike.

When students in my online course in intermediate microeconomic theory head for the bookstores, they will feel the pain of the marketplace.

The required text for the course, Jeffrey Perloff's sixth edition of *Microeconomics*, will lighten their wallets by a hefty $206.67 retail. Or $147.52 from Amazon. The book is a 20-

chapter behemoth that tips the scales at over three pounds, more than the weight of two iPads. The best deal for the students is to buy a used copy in a local bookstore and resell it at the end of the course. That option will end up costing a student about $50—one-fourth of the publisher's suggested retail price. It's the choice of about 75 percent of my students.

It's no surprise that fewer than 15 percent of students choose e-texts.

Why didn't most of the students choose the electronic version of the text? When publishers began producing e-texts they sold them for about one-half the suggested retail price of a new paper version. But students have shown a stiff resistance to buying them, mostly because they are 65-plus percent more expensive ($82.99 versus about $50 for the Perloff book) than the used paper option.

Price and Quality Keep Students Away from E-texts

Current e-texts are also a markedly inferior product. They are static PDF knockoffs of vertically oriented print pages. That means they don't display well on most computer screens, and they resist printing an easy-to-read copy by inexplicably downsizing the fonts for home printing.

Put this together with the 180-day licensing period and it's no surprise that fewer than 15 percent of students choose e-texts. (About half the students in my intermediate microeconomics course are or will become economics majors. The material in the text needs to be available for reference in future courses in the major, and possibly in graduate school.)

So far the mainstream publishing companies have shown an inability or unwillingness to produce electronic versions of K-12 or university-level textbooks that break the link with a corresponding print mode. That might be an understandable concession to navigating the book in a classroom for students operating with different versions, but it has had the important side effect of retarding the production of stand-alone texts that would exist only in digital form, and with no paper counterpart whatsoever.

Students and parents who are outraged by the high prices of textbooks should be cheering monopoly-breaking innovations in this hidebound market.

E-texts that started as a way to kill, or at least maim, the market in used paper texts actually retarded the development of new digital texts with innovative features such as audio, video and animated content under the control of the reader. Over the past five years I have sat in my office many times with publishers' sales reps who completely understood that their clay-footed bosses were wedded to the mentality of print.

It is not an uncommon story in economics to find industries with monopoly or oligopoly power using that power to slow or prevent innovation. In most cases the innovation is only delayed.

Students and parents who are outraged by the high prices of textbooks should be cheering monopoly-breaking innovations in this hidebound market.

Apple Software Could Revolutionize E-text Creation

On Jan. 19, [2012] Apple introduced new software and marketing platforms that should, within a few years, totally reshape the old ways of producing and distributing learning content. The software is called iBooks Author, and the marketing plan consists of an iBooks Store to sell e-texts for the iPad and a new version of iTunes U for delivering content directly to students.

I have created a large body of content for my students on my own, but viewing videos and other media in traditional course management systems means following internal links that open videos in separate windows, interrupting the smooth flow of logic and making efficient navigation impossible. We see the possible alternatives to this every time we see an iPod commercial or view news content on an iPad. We know that current paper and electronic texts are static. All of this is about to change.

These new texts—a term that undervalues their potential importance—can be the basis for a new art form.

Consider first the software part of Apple's package, because this is where a revolution would probably take place. What is lacking in traditional e-texts is the seamless integration of text and other media—both video and audio—and the flow and manipulation of content that the iPad and its imitators provide. But that's only part of it. The old iPad apps, as well as the newsreaders we saw in the commercials, depended on a staff of professionals who produce the digital copy that consumers eventually download.

The revolution is that ordinary users—on the order of folks who can create a PowerPoint slide deck—can now produce copy that will run on the iPad. This is revolutionary. It will unleash the creative powers of thousands of authors and artists, to say nothing of us mere mortals. Just as important, it will spawn imitators. Expect to see a Google app that will allow users to create content for Android devices.

IBooks Author allows the creation of smoothly flowing iPad "pages" of content in a mashup of text, videos, illustrations and animations that can be manipulated by the students to suit their learning needs. The software is free to everyone. Teachers can use it to produce their own content for students, customized to course objectives, but allowing the pedagogy to exploit the free-flowing navigation of an iPad. In a demonstration at Apple's news conference, we saw that an author could drag and drop an existing Word file into iBooks Author for distribution on the iPad.

These new texts—a term that undervalues their potential importance—can be the basis for a new art form. The crime novel of the future will include not only text but also videos and interactive illustrations. With iBooks Author, Apple is hoping to do what TechSmith and Camtasia Studio did for the production of videos for instruction: Put easy-to-use but powerful creative tools in the hands of ordinary people.

Camtasia Studio, by putting the tools for video creation and editing in to the hands of anyone with a computer, is now the world leader in screen-capture software. We'll see if Apple can do the same for digital books.

Required Ownership of iPads May Prove Detrimental

What are the barriers to the best-case scenario playing out for Apple? Foremost, of course, is that the plan for schools and colleges would require a near universal ownership of iPads. Colleges have achieved universal computer ownership for students, but in most cases there is no requirement for a specific brand.

Why would the major publishing companies agree to collaborate with Apple? Why would they consent to a maximum price per copy of $14.99 for K-12 texts and give Apple 30 percent of the gross? I suspect that when Apple came to them they knew the jig was up.

On the bright side, textbook authors not affiliated with the mainstream publishing companies may see the remaining 70 percent payout from publishing in the iBook Store as a handsome payoff. It is true that the publishing companies can provide marketing advantages in textbook markets, but these should be valued conservatively. A principal benefit from the iBook Store is that it is a very efficient way for prospective buyers to scan the offerings of not just one publisher, but of many.

What I would like to see is a vast increase in the quantity and diversity of instructional content in all fields. The traditional publishing companies will be hard-pressed in such an open-content world to maintain their current pricing models, and they will also be forced to compete with innovative authors who now will have drastically reduced entry barriers into the market for learning materials. Easy entry into a market sounds the death knell of monopoly, as any student of intermediate microeconomics can tell you.

7

For Now, E-texts Will Not Disrupt the Textbook Industry

John Paul Titlow

John Paul Titlow writes for ReadWriteWeb, *a technology blog. He has written for many other publications, including* The New York Times *and* Philadelphia Weekly.

The textbook industry may be in need of a revolution, but current technologies, including new e-texts, will not disrupt the industry in a meaningful way. New technologies are often too costly for students and their families who are struggling through a recession. In addition, textbook publishers are partners in the new e-text technology, so rather than being displaced by others they will maintain their position in the marketplace. Although the textbook industry is evolving and will likely look different decades from now, the technology of one company will not be responsible for this evolution.

Apple revolutionizes stuff. It's practically conventional wisdom in the tech world that, even if they're not first in the game or necessarily even the best, the Cupertino [California]-based giant has a tendency to make a noticeable impact. They didn't invent the MP3 player, smartphone or tablet, but they sure have redefined all of those products. Even if this tendency is strong, it's not necessarily always how things play out. For an example, look no further than the Apple TV.

Revolutionizing Textbooks?

Today, the company set their sights on textbooks, an industry Steve Jobs [former Apple chief executive officer] himself described as being "ripe for digital destruction." True as that may be, is what Apple planning to do in the space really all that disruptive?

Apple ultimately wants to sell more of its hardware, but if it really wants its textbook initiative to truly take off, it will have to develop apps for other platforms.

There's no doubt that giving authors dead simple tools for publishing their own interactive e-books is a big deal. As Nieman Journalism Lab's Joshua Benton so effectively outlined earlier this week [January 2012], creating a "Garage Band for e-books" could do to book publishing what the advent of the blogging platform did for short-form self-publishing on the Web. And it's also true that the immersive, interactive experience of learning from the kinds of digital textbooks Apple demoed today has far more potential than print ever did.

If the company's efforts are going to help revolutionize textbooks and education, it's going to be some time before that happens, and they're not going to do it alone.

Costly and Not Cross-Platform

Apple released the second version of its iBooks app for iOS [mobile operating system] today [January 19, 2012], which includes access to the new textbook titles. One thing the company did not announce is that the app is coming to other platforms. Granted, the iPad is still the leader of the tablet market, but Android is slowly catching up and Amazon just released a device geared toward content consumption that costs less than half of the entry level iPad. And it's growing fast.

Of course, Apple ultimately wants to sell more of its hardware, but if it really wants its textbook initiative to truly take off, it will have to develop apps for other platforms, just as Amazon has done with its Kindle apps.

Another barrier to widespread adoption of this model is the cost of the iPad. It starts at $500, which is not something every American family can afford, especially with an economy in flux. With hundreds of "pages" of content, 3D interactive graphics, embedded video and other bells and whistles, we have to imagine these books aren't particularly light on file size. As the books accumulate over time, alongside other content stored on the iPad, the 16 GB [gigabyte] entry level model may no longer cut it, making it an even more expensive investment.

Not every high school student in the United States can afford a $500 tablet device.

Not Aimed at the College Market

The cost issue might be mitigated somewhat if the initiative were not targeted exclusively at high school students.

At least for the time being, Apple's digital textbooks are targeted primarily at high school students. That fact alone presents a few roadblocks to the initiative being truly disruptive. For one, not every high school student in the United States can afford a $500 tablet device. Apple may well end up dropping the price when they launch the iPad 3 in a few weeks, but even then we're probably still talking about a several-hundred-dollar gadget. Many middle and upper class families can afford that, but kids in inner city schools and other low-income areas, some of which can barely afford enough paper textbooks, aren't going to be learning from iPads anytime soon.

For college students, investing in an iPad or similar device to replace textbooks makes simple economic sense. A single semester's worth of textbooks can easily approach the cost of an iPad. If the e-books available on the device are drastically less expensive than their paper counterparts, it would be foolish not to make the digital switch. Of course, how dramatically prices would drop remains to be seen.

The textbook is indeed one of the educational tools that is most in need of a digital makeover.

Apple Is *Partnering* with Big Publishers, Not Killing Them

College textbooks are enormously, obscenely profitable for the companies that print them. In fact, they've come up with all kinds of creative ways of milking more money out of students. Textbooks about ancient history will be revised and reissued every other semester and the company will package supplementary CD-ROM's and other digital learning materials, using them as a justification to jack up the price.

To get its new initiative off the ground, Apple is partnering with major publishers like McGraw Hill, Pearson and Houghton Mifflin Harcourt. For the high school market, perhaps those companies can afford to agree to a $15-per-book price tag. But when it comes to higher education, publishers are unlikely to allow a $180 biology print textbook be replaced with a $15 e-book. That would cut into their profits pretty dramatically. At the same time, interactive e-textbooks can't be resold once they're used, so perhaps the publishers can be convinced that their e-book revenues will be replenished on a semesterly basis without fail.

Interestingly, at the same time that Apple has unveiled major partnerships with textbooks publishers, it also unleashed what appears to be a powerful, easy-to-use publishing toolkit for producing those books. If independent authors manage to create enough competition, it's possible that bigger publishers will have no choice but to play ball with Apple's preferred pricing for textbooks.

Apple's Not the Only Player

There's little reason to doubt that a decade from now, the classroom and the tools in it will look very different from what students are accustomed to today. The textbook is indeed one of the educational tools that is most in need of a digital makeover. When paper textbooks are finally a thing of the past, it won't have been Apple's efforts alone that got us there.

For one, education is already being blown wide open by the Web. The mere concepts of "the lecture" and "the textbook" begin to look antiquated in light of things like Khan Academy, Wikipedia, Wolfram Alpha, iTunes U and MIT's [Massachusetts Institute of Technology's] Open Courseware.

Those examples are just the tip of the iceberg. You'd be hard-pressed to find a student in the U.S. today that isn't already using the Internet to supplement their educational experience to some extent. Apple is well aware of the changes that are already underway. That's why they're doing this. That's why their DIY [do-it-yourself] publishing tools include the ability to pull in pieces of the Web and incorporate HTML5 and JavaScript.

Apple is also not the first company to try to re-imagine the textbook for a digital world. The so-called "smartbooks" offered by e-textbook startup Inking are in some ways more advanced than what Apple is bringing to the table. Other companies already active in this space include Chegg and Kno, as Audrey Watters points out on Hack Education [blog].

Indeed, Apple is anything but the first entrant into this space. Not that that's stopped them in the past.

8

Free Internet-Based Education Can Change Education

Kirsten Winkler

Kirsten Winkler is a journalist, consultant, and entrepreneur who focuses on online education. Her blog, kirstenwinkler.com, is one of the leading outlets in education 2.0 and was listed by the Edublog Awards website under the category of "Best New Blog" in 2009.

The Khan Academy is using technology to have a profound impact on the way education is delivered. The organization, founded by Salman Khan in 2006, has a mission to provide a free world-class education to anyone anywhere. Khan is not supported by online ads or premiums and relies completely on donations. It is making education economically feasible for people all over the world. And Khan has taken another big step by opening its system to educators and providing tools they can use to build their own courses. This has made the organization not only popular with students but also instructors, who contribute their lessons and knowledge to the Khan Academy and in turn see their efforts assist far more people than they could in their own classrooms. In the short time since its launch, Khan Academy has over three-and-a-half million unique visitors to its site every month. Like Wikipedia before it, Khan has proven that an organization can be successful by providing information for free.

A lot has been and will be written about Salman Khan. Though he already arrived in the spotlight of mainstream media, he is clearly just at the beginning of his mission. And with fresh money in the war chest, Khan and his team are now planning the next attack on the education system.

Besides growing the faculty of the Khan Academy, Khan is planning to open the system to teachers around the globe who can then use the Knowledge Map to build their own courses and also have access to the in-depth analytic tools Khan Academy is providing at the back-end.

But here is the deal: the content must be put up to Khan Academy's noncommercial public domain. **Noncommercial**.

I believe, this is an aspect of Khan Academy most people have not thought about or didn't pay attention to yet but that has the potential to change the economics of education profoundly.

At the moment, there are basically three business models in online education. Ad-supported, freemium and premium. But there are also two large scale operations that have no business model at all, Khan Academy and Wikipedia. Let's go to the three most popular for-profit ones before we focus on the noncommercial examples.

Current Online Education Models Are Less than Ideal

Ad-supported education are in most cases smaller projects of individual educators who upload videos to YouTube and display Google ads against them. From my own experience you will earn enough money to pay for a couple of fancy coffees every month but as the revenue per click or impression for education related ads is not comparable with other topics, it is not suitable for bigger operations.

Freemium is a very popular model amongst education startups. Users have access to a big chunk of the product for free, though this part is usually also supported by display ads.

If learners then want to have access to extra content, usually grammar charts, worksheets or videos, they will have to pay.

Premium, as the name suggests, is content that is only available to paying customers. Language learning platform Babbel famously switched the popular freemium model to premium only back in November 2009 and soon afterwards announced that the startup was profitable. Another reason was the problem the team saw in displaying ads.

If you take a look at what Khan Academy is going to offer for free to educators one could ask why anyone would pay for similar products?

Ads are far from being an ideal revenue stream in an educational context. You cannot really control what is displayed next or even inside of the video lesson. Ads can be a distraction, especially when they are animated or feature sound effects and they have the draw-back that they are seen critically in a public school context and I think this is also part of Khan Academy's success amongst educators. Khan Academy has always been ad-free although nowadays Khan could make some significant income based on either Google Ads or by selling sponsorships based on his reach. 3.5 million unique visitors a month are worth a ton of money yet Khan Academy stays a noncommercial platform.

The same is of course true for Wikipedia. Jimmy Wales [co-founder of Wikipedia] is also fighting the idea of displaying advertisements or sponsored links on the site though it could earn Wikipedia a lot of money based on the page views. Yet he chooses to go in the trenches, raising money to keep Wikipedia up and running. Though Wales has no big success in getting the basic user to donate he usually meets his goal through big donations like the lastest $500k grant by Google founder Sergey Brin and his wife whereas Khan always had a steady flow of small donations to keep the Academy alive.

Khan Academy Fulfills Its Mission Free of Commercial Influence

So both, Khan and Wales, are proving that there is "a better way" to deliver true free education on the Internet. And I think this is the really radical part. If you take a look at what Khan Academy is going to offer for free to educators one could ask why anyone would pay for similar products? Khan has no commercial interest, something that resonates with the ideals of most educators. Khan is independent from big brands and publishers in education that take more and more influence in promising education startups lately by either investing and/or partnering with them.

What happens when Khan is responsible for the success of a new breed of entrepreneurs in developing countries.

One could say that at the moment Khan is "untouchable" and he and his team can do whatever they think benefits their mission. No investor can take influence in order to streamline the operation for a potential exit in 5 years like being sold to Pearson or Blackboard.

Currently, Khan Academy is supported by three big donors, Bill and Melinda Gates, Google and the O'Sullivan Foundation. I think, there is little doubt that others will follow suit in order to keep Khan Academy going for the next years. The interesting part begins when we start thinking what is going to happen when the first students will tie their financial success to what they learned for free at Khan Academy.

Universities receive large sums from their alumni every year who want to give something back to the institution that provided them with the tools to succeed in life. What happens when Khan Academy is responsible for the success of a new breed of entrepreneurs in developing countries. A recent article on *Forbes* suggests that the next Internet billionaires will come from Africa.

Free, quality education has been a dream of many educators and of course students for a long time now and Khan might be on the road to establish that mindset in the generation of users he and his faculty are teaching every day.

9

Students with Disabilities Benefit from Digital Books

Nirvi Shah

Nirvi Shah is a reporter for Education Week *who covers special education, school nutrition, health, safety, and bullying. Prior to joining* Education Week, *Shah was a reporter for the* Miami Herald.

Digital booksharing illustrates how technology can be a powerful partner in education. Bookshare is a free service offered to students with disabilities that has made a remarkable difference in their lives by broadening access to printed materials. It uses advances in digital media to speed up the creation of audiobooks. Prior to Bookshare, audio book production was a cumbersome process, which meant it was months before material was available to students and teachers. Thousands of students with print disabilities use Bookshare to keep up with their classwork and to enjoy reading more.

When 4th grade teacher Heather Whitby sat down for a book discussion last week with a group of students at her Bethesda, Md., elementary school, other students read on their own, including two who a year ago might not have been able to do so.

Because of their disabilities, Kyle Nordheimer and Maurice Van Lowe struggle with traditional printed text. But, using Bookshare, a nonprofit that provides free electronic copies of books to students with certain disabilities, both boys watched computer screens scroll through the text of *The Chocolate Touch*, listening to it at the same time.

Inspired by Napster, the music-sharing service, Bookshare turns books into a format that can be read aloud by computers, magnified, and spaced differently so that students with vision problems or learning disabilities can read them. They're even available at the same time new releases reach bookstore shelves, unlike typical audiobooks.

Its services are an example of how e-book technology, taking off with consumers, has powerful potential for students who previously relied on more cumbersome and more difficult-to-obtain alternatives to the traditional book.

For schoolchildren, Bookshare is free, underwritten by a $32 million infusion from the U.S. Department of Education four years ago that's led to 150,000 student Bookshare memberships across the nation.

Typically, students who can't read traditional books begin falling behind on the first day of school.

And the department's office of special education programs gave the Palo Alto [California]-based organization another $3 million in mid-October [2011] to take its work even further during the next year. With this one-year Leveraging Impact Through Technology grant project—shortened, aptly, to LIT— Bookshare will create free e-book readers for Android phones, a free Web-based e-book reader, a virtual bookshelf that student members can use from anywhere, and access to Bookshare materials in mp3 and other audio formats.

"We know we need people to be able to read the books in more ways," said Betsy Beaumon, the vice president of literacy and general manager of the 10-year-old Bookshare. "We're all about, 'How do we use technology to make doing this cheaper and faster?' When you think about education, that's critical. When a student needs a book, they need a book."

After the 3,500-student Brewster Central district in New York started using Bookshare about 3[frac12] years ago, "the difference to teachers, anecdotally, was amazing," said Donna Schneider, the assistive-technology specialist. Students who once found reading to be a chore, she said, "started saying, 'I want to read this other book on my own.' They want to read."

Instead of text being a source of information or inspiration, it's too often been the cause of frustration.

Bookshare Offers an Alternative to Printed Materials

Typically, students who can't read traditional books begin falling behind on the first day of school.

Unable to learn at all from the ubiquitous printed materials at school, or hampered because they learn more slowly than their peers, such students often have had to wait months until audiobooks became available, or depend on a school employee to deconstruct a particular text, scan it, and convert it into a digital file to be read aloud by the right software. An alternative is for students to use special, sometimes unwieldy, equipment they lug from class to class that magnifies the words in class worksheets and books or work with an aide.

Instead of text being a source of information or inspiration, it's too often been the cause of frustration.

"They fell behind and became frustrated through no fault of their own," Kerri Larkin, the director of academic programs in the office of special education for the District of Columbia school system, said of those students.

Near the end of last school year, the 45,000-student district decided to arrange for a Bookshare membership for students with print disabilities—a range of conditions that hinder the ability to read words in a book or on paper. As eligible students' education plans are updated, Bookshare memberships will be added to them, Ms. Larkin said.

[Bookshare] has agreements with about 160 publishers, which send the nonprofit an electronic version of a book as soon as it is published.

Before Bookshare, Carlos Zacarias walked around school with a device that resembles an overhead projector. Mr. Zacarias, a junior at the district's Woodrow Wilson High School who has low vision, would place reading material at the bottom and it would be magnified on an attached screen.

"It really got on my nerves. I had to move from class to class" with the device, he said. Now, he sports a laptop he can use to log in to Bookshare from any class, a change that doesn't advertise his disability the way the bulky equipment did.

Cooperation with Publishers Helps Speed the Process

Produced by nonprofit groups, commercial publishers, and the Library of Congress, audiobooks take longer to reach schools because they typically involve someone going into a studio and reading a book aloud.

Bookshare's process is much faster, Ms. Beaumon said. The organization has agreements with about 160 publishers, which send the nonprofit an electronic version of a book as soon as it is published.

"We get an electronic feed from our publishers the same time [a book] is hitting Amazon, the same time it's hitting iTunes," Ms. Beaumon said. Instead of using human voices, Bookshare book voices are computer-generated, with a robotic sound somewhere between KITT from the "Knight Rider" television series and R2D2 from "Star Wars."

When Mr. Zacarias needs to rest his eyes, he can listen to books on his laptop computer, said Roxanne Richardson, one of the district's vision teachers.

Bookshare memberships are for students who are blind, have low vision, have such learning disabilities as severe dyslexia, or have a disability such as cerebral palsy that could keep them from holding a book. Such students have what are collectively called print disabilities—a distinct departure from saying "learning disabilities," said David Rose, the chief education officer at the Center for Applied Special Technology, or CAST, in Wakefield, Mass.

Using the phrase "print disability" said Mr. Rose, "is co-locating the problem. Print is part of the problem." His non-profit organization works on expanding learning opportunities for all individuals, especially those with disabilities, through a set of principles called "universal design for learning."

"We can convey that information in a whole host of ways now. In that world, you go, 'Print is not very good for a lot of kids,'" he said.

Bookshare has amassed more than 125,000 titles for students to download, and the nonprofit takes requests when its library doesn't hold something a student needs.

As evidence of the growing need for text that reads itself, Ms. Beaumon notes that many tablet computers, including the iPad, are built with the ability to read text aloud.

Aside from publishers, Bookshare also gets electronic copies of books from the National Instructional Materials Access Center, a federal repository of textbooks in Frankfort, Ky., that was created under federal special education law.

In most cases, states and school districts adopting new textbooks must require publishers to create and submit electronic copies of the books they are buying to the database in a specific format.

Respect for Copyright Is Important and Carefully Guarded

Whether from publishers or the federal textbook repository, those electronic copies of books can't be used by individuals. They must first be converted into a usable format by Bookshare and others. Bookshare has amassed more than 125,000 titles for students to download, and the nonprofit takes requests when its library doesn't hold something a student needs.

Books and other copyright material provided through Bookshare and other organizations using an amendment to the copyright law must be guarded closely. Only students with proof of a qualifying disability can use the free Bookshare books, Ms. Beaumon said. The organization also has a fee-based service for adults.

Every book downloaded has its own digital fingerprint to ensure it is used for just one student. Even if a teacher has a half-dozen students in a class who qualify, each of their books must be acquired separately for each student.

John King, a junior at Walt Whitman High School in Bethesda, Md., who has a learning disability, said on his own it may take him four minutes to read a single page of a book, making homework time-consuming. Before he learned about Bookshare in 8th grade, any assignments that involved a lot of reading crowded out the others, and sometimes went undone.

"I'm definitely enjoying the reading a lot more," said Mr. King. "It was just such an improvement from taking hours to taking an hour or less."

Before joining Bookshare, the Montgomery County, Md., school district where he is enrolled created its own version of electronic books, said Linda Wilson, who oversees technology for high-incidence disabilities in the nearly 147,000-student district. For some titles, the district still does.

Using Bookshare is much faster, Ms. Wilson said, although the district has had to devote many hours of training to explain what it is and how to use it. Teachers have to be educated on the technical side of using Bookshare as well as the copyright laws involved.

Part of the latest federal grant for Bookshare will be devoted to a partnership with the American Institutes of Research, a Washington-based research group, to provide free professional development to increase the use of Bookshare.

New Advances in Technology Will Remove Remaining Barriers

Barriers with printed materials remain, even when they are converted into Bookshare and other formats. For example, many textbooks are filled with photographs, diagrams, charts, and drawings that may be accompanied by a single line or two of text. While electronic books will read aloud that simple description, more elaborate explanations aren't available in most cases. Bookshare plans to provide more description and is working with volunteers who donate time describing images in books, Ms. Beaumon said.

Mr. Rose, of CAST, said such difficulties with current forms of e-books underscore the need to keep advancing new media.

You don't notice print as a disabling material until we have alternatives, he said. "We need the best medium possible to teach you—that's what we ask."

10

Apps Can Help Special Needs Students Improve Social Skills

Rick Dean

Rick Dean is a journalist and online editor for The Topeka Capital-Journal.

An application developed for older children with Asperger's Syndrome could prove to be a valuable tool for navigating social interactions with their peers. The new app, called "Sosh", offers a wide range of activities such as a slang dictionary, exercises in relaxation and conversational skills, and a voice meter that a child can use to determine how loud he is talking. The developers believe that technology is the most effective way to reach out to the pre-teen and teen sets, who are often no longer receiving the level of support they did at an earlier age and, as such, can struggle in the more social environment of middle school and high school.

The junior high-aged kids are talking typical teenage smack during lunch when one jokingly tells another to go jump in a lake.

The youngster on the receiving end of the mild putdown looks puzzled.

"Why would I do that?," he responds. "I can't swim."

The group erupts with laughter, and the teen with Asperger's Syndrome—a disorder on the Autism spectrum characterized by significant difficulties in social interaction—walks away hurt, his embarrassment obvious.

Mark Bowers knows of many such encounters through his work as a pediatric psychologist. A University of Kansas [KU] and Topeka-trained clinician now practicing in Brighton, Mich., northwest of Detroit, Bowers has spent his career helping children, adolescents and young adults with social anxieties or development disorders deal with everyday situations they struggle to comprehend.

"These are kids who often are highly verbal, usually have pretty high IQs and do well academically," he said of his Asperger students. "They also are kids who want to be social with others, but their brains are just not quite wired to understand social cues."

Knowing that many of his students deal better with a computer than with a teacher or therapist, Bowers and his wife Kelly—also a licensed psychologist—turned to technology for a teaching aid.

Asperger's Syndrome is a lifetime disorder, though many people learn to handle its symptoms as they grow into adulthood.

They developed and released Sosh, a mobile-device application designed, in the words of its iTunes description, "to help tweens, teens and young adults improve social skills." The program currently is compatible only with iPhones and iPads.

Among its some 60 pages of instructive, interactive features is the "What Did That Mean?" program in which a student can enter a slang phrase he could not comprehend—"Go jump in a lake"—and learn he was being advised to back away as opposed to actually getting wet. Other parts of the program let a student archive notes about how he felt upon hearing the comment, how he reacted and what he might do differently upon hearing it again.

"It's that very literal interpretation of a phrase that makes these kids end up getting teased or ridiculed or made to feel awkward," Bowers explained. "Their peers can't understand why they're interpreting everything so literally."

Asperger's Syndrome is a lifetime disorder, though many people learn to handle its symptoms as they grow into adulthood. The tunnel-vision tendency to focus on things that appeal only to the patient—as opposed to showing an interest in the activities of peers—is a characteristic that can be both positive and negative. Researchers today believe people who dealt with Asperger's at an early age included Wolfgang Mozart, Albert Einstein, Madam Currie and Thomas Jefferson.

Helping people deal at a young age is critical and the purpose of Sosh, Bowers said.

"We have to teach kids in the way they learn best, and this generation seems to deal well with technology," he said.

Helping Teens Interpret Social Cues

The app is designed for a slightly older audience for whom social interaction disabilities are a particular concern.

"We felt the older kids were being left out, especially those on the Autism spectrum," Bowers said. "They get a lot of attention and early intervention when they're young, but then we put them in school and hope they learn through support programs. We think (Sosh) is something sleek and stylish and cool for older kids that was missing in the market."

Sosh is considerably more than a slang dictionary.

In sub-menus built around five Rs on the home page—relate, recognize, regulate, reason, relax—users can find exercises to help develop conversational skills: how to maintain eye contact, how far away to stand in a conversation, how to be a good listener. As some Asperger students tend to speak loudly, there is a Voice Meter—similar to the volume level displayed in basketball arenas—that shows a student how loud he is talking. There are relaxation techniques, both audio and visual, that can be helpful to a wide group of people.

"Parents tell us these exercises are helpful to them after a day of being stressed out from dealing with their kids with special needs," said Kelly Bowers, a KU grad who did her psychology residency at Topeka's VA [US Department of Veterans Affairs] hospital.

The app has value for more than just Asperger students, noted Mark Bowers, who worked at Topeka's Menninger Clinic before entering the Masters program in clinical psychology at Washburn and the residency program in child psychology at the University of Kansas Medical Center.

"We created the app with Asperger's students in mind," he explained, "but some treatments overlap for students with ADHD [Attention Deficit Hyperactivity Distorder] or social anxiety disorders, or people who are just shy."

11

Robots Help Autistic Children Learn

Chris Woolston

Chris Woolston is a writer and editor who specializes in science, health, and travel. His "Healthy Skeptic" column appears every other Monday in the Los Angeles Times. Woolston's work has recently appeared in Reader's Digest, Prevention, Men's Health, and the AARP Bulletin.

University researchers in California and England are using robots to help children with autism develop skills to interact with other people. The robots have been designed to have some human features, making them appealing to children, and enable autistic children in particular to practice their social skills. Research on the effectiveness of this new use of robotic technology is scant but initial results have been promising, offering the potential for another tool to encourage communication and cooperation competencies in autistic children.

Robots aren't known for their soft side. They build cars and defuse bombs; they don't, as a rule, make friends or deal with feelings. But a few groups of researchers around the world are working to build robots for an unusual purpose: Making emotional connections with autistic children who often struggle to interact with humans.

There's something about machines that really seems to resonate with many kids with autism, says Maja Mataric, co-director of the Robotics Research Lab at USC [University of Southern California]. These children often have trouble reading human emotions and social cues—complexities they don't have to worry about when they're around a mechanical being.

"Robots are simpler than people," Mataric says.

Still, robots may seem like unlikely candidates for a job usually filled by therapists. As Mataric points out, the general public usually thinks of robots as either cold and efficient workers (at their best) or outright evil beings bent on enslaving humanity (at their worst).

Therapy Robots Include Some Human Features

The researchers at USC have a different vision. "We're trying to create something that's endearing," Mataric says.

The result: Bandit, a metallic-colored, child-sized robot that can win the attention—and even empathy—of hard-to-reach kids.

Bandit has a pleasant, inviting face with a movable mouth, archable eyebrows and camera eyes that let him "watch" his playmates. He also has proximity sensors to gauge whether kids are backing away or moving in. If they get too close, he can wheel away.

With Bandit's encouragement, children have learned how to take turns and initiate play with others.

With his motor-driven arms, Bandit can automatically mimic the motions of children and lead a game of Simon Says. He can make sad sighs or happy chips, and he blows bubbles with the push of a button. He can also talk in soothing tones, although USC researches are just beginning to use Bandit's speech in their work with children with autism.

Bandit, who has been around in various incarnations since 2007, is human-ish but still obviously a machine, which is exactly the look that Mataric and colleagues were aiming for. If he looked too much like a robot, kids wouldn't want to be his friend. And if he looked too human, he would likely make kids with autism feel intimidated and overwhelmed. "It was a balance that we had to find," she says.

So far, a few dozen kids with autism spectrum disorders have spent time with Bandit in various small studies. Mataric would like to have more kids visit, but she says it's hard to find children and families who are willing and able to complete a study. Still, she has seen some real signs of progress. With Bandit's encouragement, children have learned how to take turns and initiate play with others. Bandit has even inspired some children to smile socially for the first time, she says.

Bandit has an overseas soulmate of sorts in KASPAR, a robot who works with kids with autism in a lab at the University of Hertfordshire in England.

With his baseball cap, black hair and child-like face, KASPAR (the name is an acronym for Kinesics and Synchronisation in Personal Assistant Robotics) looks more like an oversized doll than a robot. But he's still a big hit among the autistic.

While not every child is interested in KASPAR, "we've had a lot of successes over the years," says senior research fellow Ben Robins, who has been working with the robot for five years.

Robins has heard from parents and teachers that kids who always seemed to be locked in their own worlds suddenly showed an interest in other people after spending time with KASPAR. "I can't say for sure that the robot is responsible," he adds.

Unlike Bandit, KASPAR doesn't run automatically; a nearby researcher guides his actions with a remote control. Robins acknowledges that the bot isn't as advanced as Bandit or many other robots out there. But that suits him just fine. "I'm working from the standpoint of the children, not the technology," he says.

In the years since he first helped design the robot in 2006, Robins says he has removed features to make the robot simpler and easier to play with. "Children need something basic that is both reliable and repetitive. Everything else is already so confusing to them."

Machines . . . may be able to help 'bridge the gap' between children with autism and the outside world.

Robins envisions eventually building 15 or so KASPARs that schools or hospitals could keep for long-term therapy. Likewise, Mataric can picture a time when families could buy a Bandit or similar bot of their own to use at home.

For now, both goals are hampered by a lack of funding. Mataric says take-home Bandits could be a reality within five years if a venture capitalist would step up, but so far she isn't exactly swamped with offers.

Another challenge is that Mataric, Robins and other researchers lack the resources necessary to run the sort of large-scale clinical trials that could answer some key questions: How long do the benefits of therapy last? How do the social skills learned in the lab translate to the real world? Which children are most likely to benefit? And how can researchers design robots to get the best results with the fewest setbacks?

Resources Are Lacking for Research into the Robots' Effectiveness

"Rigorous studies have to be conducted," says Zachary Warren, an assistant professor of pediatrics and director of the Treatment and Research Institute for Autism Spectrum Disorders at Vanderbilt University in Nashville. "That's how technology proves its worth."

Warren has participated in small-scale research projects involving robots and children with autism. In April [2011], he was the lead author of an article in the journal *Pediatrics* that evaluated a wide range of therapies for young children with autism. While many treatments out there have little scientific merit and no real track record for success, Warren sees real promise in the robotic approach. Machines, he says, may be able to help "bridge the gap" between children with autism and the outside world.

But robots aren't for everybody. Some children are profoundly disinterested or even flat-out afraid of the beings, Mataric says. "Some kids aren't going to engage, and that's fine," she says.

In other cases, kids engage only too well, Robins says. Children can get very possessive of KASPAR, which defeats the goal of learning to cooperate and take turns. Robins also worries that some children could become overly attached to their robotic friend.

"At the end of the day, it's just a machine," Robins says. "The ultimate goal is encouraging interaction with other people."

12

Data-Driven Schools See Rising Scores

John Hechinger

John Hechinger is a reporter for Bloomberg News. *Prior to working at* Bloomberg, *he was a reporter for* The Wall Street Journal.

High-tech strategies are increasingly being employed by school districts to improve student academic performance. Many districts such as Montgomery County, Maryland, Public Schools now rely on data collection, much of it in real time, to drive instruction and boost achievement. The district has poured millions of dollars into the technology needed to reach its goals. Montgomery officials credit their focus on data as having helped close persistent achievement gaps between white and minority students in the early grades. But critics, including some parents, claim that the fallout from this approach should be considered. They assert that the achievement gap in part has been closed by a drop in achievement levels at the top end of the scale as less focus and money has been directed to the district's middle-class schools. In addition, they contend, excessive testing and tracking of results through a centralized database has meant there is less time for creative work and project style learning, which is just as essential to a child's education as doing well on tests.

Last fall [2008], high-school senior Duane Wilson started getting D's on assignments in his Advanced Placement [AP] history, psychology and literature classes. Like a smoke detector sensing fire, a school computer sounded an alarm.

The Edline system used by the Montgomery County, Md., Public Schools emailed each poor grade to his mother as soon as teachers logged it in. Coretta Brunton, Duane's mother, sat her son down for a stern talk. Duane hit the books and began earning B's. He is headed to Atlanta's Morehouse College in the fall.

If it hadn't been for the tracking system, says the 17-year-old, "I might have failed and I wouldn't be going to college next year."

Montgomery, a suburb of Washington, D.C., spends $47 million a year on technology like Edline. It is at the vanguard of what is known as the "data-driven" movement in U.S. education—an approach that builds on the heavy testing of President George W. Bush's No Child Left Behind law. Using district-issued Palm Pilots, for instance, teachers can pull up detailed snapshots of each student's progress on tests and other measures of proficiency.

The high-tech strategy, which uses intensified assessments and the real-time collection of test scores, grades and other data to identify problems and speed up interventions, has just received a huge boost from President Barack Obama and Education Secretary Arne Duncan.

The 139,000-student district ... says the strategy has helped it nearly close an achievement gap between white and minority students in the early grades.

The Obama economic stimulus plan provides $100 billion for schools over the next two years, almost doubling the federal education budget. To qualify for much of the money, states will have to provide data showing progress in student achievement—giving the edge to districts such as Montgomery that already have systems in place.

Because of the new incentives, systems similar to Montgomery's are expected to spread around the country. A look at the district's experience reveals the promise and potential pitfalls of the data-driven approach.

At the county school system's Office of Shared Accountability, 40 employees generate reports on such indicators as how many students take algebra in middle school or the SAT [college admission exam] in high school. Principals, in turn, study schoolwide reports from the district's databanks to detect patterns of failing grades. Alerts of flagging performance come from Edline and another data-tracking system modeled after one used by the New York City police. The warnings, often sent via email, can spark immediate action, such as afterschool tutoring, study sessions and meetings with families.

Closing the Gap

The 139,000-student district, one of the nation's largest, says the strategy has helped it nearly close an achievement gap between white and minority students in the early grades. It also says the system has enabled it to identify minorities with academic gifts earlier, vaulting many more into demanding AP classes.

Mr. Duncan says Montgomery is a model in using data to spur improvement. "They're doing a tremendous amount right," the education secretary says, noting that the system is one of only a handful in the nation that tracks the college completion rate of its graduates. Montgomery's data system should be "the norm, not the exception," he says.

A computer system, using scores on Preliminary SAT admissions tests, flags students, often minorities, who have academic gifts but aren't enrolled in challenging courses.

But a group called the Parents Coalition of Montgomery County questions the millions of dollars spent on technology. The group says the system's emphasis on closing the achievement gap between whites and minorities has shortchanged gifted students and those with disabilities. The parents also complain that the frequent use of standardized tests, beginning in grade school, stifles creativity and is crowding out the arts.

Robert Schaeffer, public education director of the National Center for Fair & Open Testing, which has been a longtime critic of standardized assessments, echoes those concerns. He says school districts like Montgomery risk neglecting broader holistic measures of critical thinking that can't easily be tracked on a database. "Education is narrowed to little more than a test," he says.

Kindergarten Scores

District officials largely dismiss such criticisms and credit the system with a number of successes. For the past two years, almost 90% of kindergartners ended the year able to read a basic text proficiently on a standardized assessment, with only marginal differences among races and income groups. Seven years ago, just 52% of African-American students, 42% of Latinos, and 44% of low-income students reached that benchmark.

Montgomery has also succeeded in pushing more students to take rigorous AP classes, an important factor in admissions at selective colleges. A computer system, using scores on Preliminary SAT admissions tests, flags students, often minorities, who have academic gifts but aren't enrolled in challenging courses. Principals and teachers then encourage those children to sign up.

Over the past decade, the number of African-American students who achieved a passing or higher score on at least one AP test rose to 1,152 from 199. For Hispanic students, the figure increased to 1,336 from 218. The number of white and Asian-American students passing the exam rose, too, though not as dramatically.

Some evidence shows that progress on the achievement gap may dissipate over time. In eighth grade, about 90% of white and Asian students tested proficient or advanced in math on state tests, compared with only half of African-Americans and Hispanics. SAT scores of white and Asian-American students averaged more than 1700, compared with 1336 for African-Americans and 1401 for Hispanics.

Superintendent Jerry Weast acknowledges the system has much work left to do. He says the system's accomplishments are impressive only when compared with what he considers poor results elsewhere in the U.S. Dr. Weast, the son of Kansas farmers, likes to tell staffers: "We are a tall tree in a short forest."

Green Zone, Red Zone

When Dr. Weast became superintendent in 1999, he raised an alarm by forecasting a coming crisis in Montgomery County. He saw two districts: a "green zone" that was mainly white and wealthy and a "red zone" that was largely poor, black and Latino, with many students who spoke English as a second language. The low-achieving, low-income population was growing fast, threatening to skew the system's overall progress, he argued.

Dr. Weast focused first on giving poor children a leg up in early grades. He pushed the school district to spend an additional $60 million annually on red-zone elementary schools. Green-zone schools get $13,000 per student, compared with $15,000 in the red zone, the district says. Classes in red-zone schools have only 15 students in kindergarten and 17 in first and second grades—compared with 25 and 26 in the green zone. Dr. Weast also started all-day kindergarten, first in the red zone and then throughout the district.

"Red zone" Highland Elementary, in Silver Spring, has seen some of the most dramatic gains. Five years ago, the school's academic results were so poor that it was on the verge of a state takeover. More than 80% of students at the school are eligible for the federal lunch program—a standard measure of poverty—and 62% speak English as their second language. In December [2008], Highland won a Maryland "blue ribbon" award as a school among the state's top 10% academically. About 92% of Highland fifth-graders were rated proficient or advanced on state reading and math tests last year—above state averages.

For five years, each Highland instructor has kept a "running record" of student results on reading assessments, either on a Palm Pilot or a paper checklist. Not all teachers, though, have embraced the system. Bonnie Cullison, president of the Montgomery County Education Association, the main teachers' union, estimates that such data-recording efforts add about three to four hours to teachers' weekly workloads. So far, 11 of 33 teachers at Highland have either left the system or are teaching in other Montgomery schools.

"This is a lot of hard work," says Principal Raymond Myrtle. "A lot of teachers don't want to do it. For those who don't like it, we suggested they do something else."

Adrian's mother, Carmen Perez, who speaks Spanish at home, says her son couldn't write his own name when he began kindergarten. Now, he reads on a first-grade level.

On a recent morning, fifth-grade teacher Robin Weber sat with a small group of students, showing them flashcards with vocabulary. "What's this word?" she asked Natalie Somkhoyai, 10, the child of Thai immigrants. "Essential," she said slowly. "Very good!" Ms. Weber said.

Based on Ms. Weber's data entries, Natalie was found to need extra help with reading comprehension, so she spent a period in the "intervention room" that afternoon with teacher Tracey Witthaus. There, Natalie and a small group of children read a passage about a forest fire at Yellowstone National Park.

"I want you to summarize," Ms. Witthaus said—why do people need to evacuate? Natalie had the answer: "There's too much smoke."

In another classroom, 6-year-old kindergartner Adrian Perez, a son of Salvadoran immigrants, read a passage about a caterpillar while his teacher Jordana Oginz recorded his progress with the stylus of a Palm Pilot. Adrian confused the word "said" for "some." He dropped the "s" at the end of words like "shells" and "comes." At the end of the day, Ms. Oginz consulted her hand-held computer. The device calculated that Adrian read the text with 95% accuracy. Ms. Oginz planned to place Adrian in a small group with children who needed similar extra help. "I can pinpoint exactly what they need to learn," Ms. Oginz said.

Adrian's mother, Carmen Perez, who speaks Spanish at home, says her son couldn't write his own name when he began kindergarten. Now, he reads on a first-grade level. "I want him to go to college," says Ms. Perez, a secretary married to a house painter.

Other parents, meanwhile, have expressed concern that the data-driven system unfairly diverts resources from more middle-class "green" schools into the "red zone."

Parents Coalition member Heidi Dubin says her children's elementary classes in a green-zone school were too large and focused on meeting proficiency standards. She says her older daughter was advanced and could read Shakespeare in third grade, and was "learning nothing" in Montgomery schools. "You close the gap if the bottom comes up"—but also if "the top comes down," says Ms. Dubin, an international tax-planning specialist.

Melissa Landa, a former Montgomery elementary-school teacher who is now a visiting professor at the University of Maryland, says "the amount of testing is really excessive" in Montgomery schools. "And if teachers aren't testing, they are preparing kids for testing." She believes that elementary-school children in the district should spend more time on projects and creative work and less time drilling.

Focus on Testing

School officials say the amount of testing isn't necessarily more than many other districts. The district contends that its ability to systematically track test results through its huge centralized databases helps to pace both students and teachers.

Dr. Weast, the superintendent, makes no apologies about spending disproportionately on poor elementary schools, saying that children often arrive with severe deficits that must be addressed.

To boost students who underperform on tests, the district gives them a double dose of English and mathematics, often instead of electives such as music and art—another initiative the parents' coalition has criticized.

Some parents are angry about a plan that is phasing out special centers for students with disabilities. As part of a national movement known as mainstreaming, they are instead being taught in regular classes. Bob Astrove, parent of a son with a learning disability, says his child flourished in the separate centers—and just finished his junior year in college. "He needed the small, controlled environment," says Mr. Astrove, who claims the district is shutting down the centers in part to shift money to its green-zone initiatives.

Gifted students, say school officials, have plenty of challenges, through extra work in class. The district says it is now spending more on special education, not less, because students receive extra supports in regular classrooms. Administrators also say they get few complaints from parents of children who get double doses of academic subjects. The district tries, when possible, to preserve electives such as art and music classes using an extended-day program.

Dr. Weast, the superintendent, makes no apologies about spending disproportionately on poor elementary schools, saying that children often arrive with severe deficits that must be addressed. "Those who need more get more," he says.

13

Student Data Systems May Give Parents Too Much Information

Allison Gilbert

Allison Gilbert writes regularly for the Huffington Post. *She has been featured on ABC, CBS, CNN, and* Extra! *Gilbert is the author of* Parentless Parents: How the Loss of Our Mothers and Fathers Impacts the Way We Raise Our Children.

Schools and teachers are using student management systems to keep parents informed of their child's progress. In these systems, grades, assignments, and daily activities are all available to parents online. But many parents and students feel the use of these tools is excessive and encroaches on the child's privacy and autonomy. Furthermore, relationships are negatively impacted when parents are perceived as policing from a distance. While parental involvement is necessary and encouraged, some kids feel that the intense level of micromanaging undermines their confidence and creates tension among family members.

A re schools creating a new breed of helicopter parent?

Teacher Terri Reh wants parents to monitor their children's entire educational career online.

"I post all my students' responsibilities, their current and upcoming assignments, and timelines for every project they have," says the teacher at Flagstaff Academy in Longmont,

Colorado. "I also post messages detailing the status of homework, whether it's missing, late, or incomplete."

Reh refers to herself as her school's "biggest technology adopter," and recently won a statewide award for her efforts.

Unlike many teachers across the country who use school-funded technology to help middle and high school students track their own work online, Reh uses it to target parents. Her students are in third grade.

"Anything we can do to engage parents is what we need to do. Kids do better in school when mom and dad are involved," Reh says.

Reh also has a website highlighting her daily classroom schedule and invites parents to subscribe to her Twitter feed so they can follow her activities in and out of the classroom.

Patricia Davis' daughter is in Reh's class. The mother of twins enjoys going on Infinite Campus, the centralized computer system Flagstaff uses, any time of the day or night.

Online programs have expanded to such a degree parents can now conduct full academic surveillance.

"I use it to make sure my daughter's assignments are done and to check her overall grades. I've sometimes caught mistakes when the grade online doesn't reflect the grade I know she earned, but when I've brought these errors to the teacher's attention, she's corrected them every time."

Student management systems, as they are known in the educational world, began trickling into U.S. schools about 10 years ago. They are now so popular Ann Flynn, director of Education Technology at the National School Boards Association, considers their use "commonplace."

In its latest study released last year, the educational marketing company Market Data Retrieval concluded that 97% of all districts it surveyed have "substantially or fully implemented" some sort of student data management system.

Indeed, online programs have expanded to such a degree parents can now conduct full academic surveillance.

Much of this e-hovering happens in real-time without the need for a child to share potentially disappointing news at the dinner table. If your son gets a C on a quiz, you could get pinged with an automated e-mail before he gets home from school and can tell you himself.

Carol Bengle Gilbert (no relation to author) wants none of it. The Maryland mother of three children ages 16, 13 and 11 says the amount of information coming at her is out of control and unnecessary.

She says her children's teachers not only post assignments and due dates, they also list the percentage each assignment is worth toward final grades.

When questions come up about how her kids are doing in school, teachers have assumed she's been following along online.

"I tell them flat out, I don't do that. I don't think it's normal to be so involved. It creates an unhealthy relationship between parents and their kids. I think kids resent it. My job as a parent is to teach them how to do things on their own. I don't want to be that kind of policeman in my house."

On Edutopia.org, the George Lucas Educational Foundation website, kids have been vocal for years about wanting more autonomy in school.

One child complained on a discussion board, "Every single time a teacher entered a grade incorrectly, I had a missing assignment, or something else bringing my grade in a certain class down, it was hell at home. I began to stress more over my parents' reaction to grades than the actual grades."

Another student railed, "My mom now seems like the enemy."

Christopher Daddis, an expert in adolescent-parent relationships and associate professor of psychology at The Ohio State University, says while children almost always get better grades when parents participate in their education, kids run into emotional trouble if they feel micromanaged.

"When parents exert too much control, children can become depressed and have increased levels of anxiety."

Tensions also bubble up when students feel blindsided. Daddis says parents who choose to keep tabs on their children's schoolwork remotely must come clean.

"It's important to recognize that parents have the upper hand like never before. They can know something a child hasn't shared and catch them in a lie.

"Parents need to inform their children that they are going online, and tell them honestly why they feel they need to do so. They should never go behind their child's back."

14

The All-Digital Library Embraces an Electronic Future

Bridget McCrea

Bridget McCrea is a business and technology writer in Clearwater, Florida. Her articles have been published in Fortune Small Business, Black Enterprise, Hispanic Magazine, *and* Inc. Business Resources, *as well as on the* Wall Street Journal's *Real EstateJournal.com and CareerJournal.com.*

School libraries around the country are expanding their traditional purpose and embracing technology to enhance their available services. But the Cushing Academy in Massachusetts has gone a step further and become all-digital, replacing most of its physical book collection with electronic resources. Although library traditionalists criticize such a drastic move, Academy officials defend their choice and point out the benefits of going all-digital. The new format allows the library to purchase only what students request, when they need it—saving the expense of guessing what books to purchase with the potential result of wasting funds on unused materials. By using e-readers, the library has increased available titles from the 40,000 books previously on its shelves to closer to one million titles now only a download away. But the move has not been without challenges. Matching e-books to compatible hardware and keeping the technology current have proven difficult but doable, and the long-term advantages, the Academy feels, will outweigh these obstacles.

Two years ago, Cushing Academy of Ashburnham, MA, made a bold move when it got rid of Fisher-Watkins Library's 40,000 books and replaced them with electronic sources. During the overhaul all resources were converted to digital formats, and the library's Web site was redesigned to provide students and faculty with online resources and tools on a 24/7 basis.

Tom Corbett, the library's executive director, said the sweeping change was part of the 450-student Cushing Academy's commitment to becoming a national leader in 21st century secondary education. "We wanted to create a library that reflected the reality of how students conduct research and that fostered what they do," said Corbett. "We needed a facility that went beyond the 'stacks' and embraced the digital future."

Prior to the revamping Corbett said the library was well stocked with printed books and a database collection. "It wasn't a neglected library by any stretch. However, like a lot of high school libraries, it wasn't what the administration or library staff wanted," said Corbett. "The opportunity to change the library dynamics surfaced, so the school's leaders decided to take it."

Additions included new LCD screens that show CNN news and that display book covers of new titles that students and faculty might be interested in.

Existing Books Relocated or Donated to Area Libraries

Funded internally with the private school's capital funds, the project kicked off with the sale of the library's physical collection. "We had to find new homes for the books and clear the shelves," said Corbett, who was hired in 2009 to oversee the process and run the new library. Books were offered to school departments first and the rest were donated to area libraries.

The undertaking whittled Fisher-Watkins Library's collection down to about 10,000 books. Most of the remaining titles left were either contributed by donors or were art or poetry books. "Neither of those subject areas translate well electronically," Corbett explained, adding that the physical collection will not be expanded unless a specific book isn't available in electronic format.

Cushing Academy then hired an architect to redesign the library. The building already had ample "open space," according to Corbett, but needed more steps, doors, furniture, and a cafe where students and faculty could mingle and collaborate. An existing computer lab was converted into a lounge for faculty and staff, new WiFi access points were added, and new electric boxes were installed to accommodate student laptop use in the building. The library also set up a Drupal-based content management system that runs its online catalog and physical circulation setup.

Other additions included new LCD screens that show CNN news and that display book covers of new titles that students and faculty might be interested in. Electronic books were the final piece of the puzzle. After testing out both the Sony Reader and Amazon Kindle the school decided to use a combination of both devices. Students and teachers can also access the books through the library's Web site and read it on their laptops, desktops, and tablets.

Digital Services Expand Access to Resources

Cushing Academy signed up for a "pay as you use it" arrangement with EB Library (EBL), the library division of ebooks .com, to populate portable reading devices with texts. The service has more than 200,000 academic, copyrighted e-books from university presses and other sources.

"We wanted to get out of the 'purchase the books up front and hope someone uses them' mentality," Corbett explained.

"With our new system we can provide access to a much larger set of resources that are paid for as they are used."

Students and teachers search through Fisher-Watkins Library's digital catalog and select one or more texts. The system automatically checks the materials out for the user, and then the school is charged when the materials are used.

"This opens up access to many [more] resources than we could ever manage with a paper-based approach," said Corbett. "Our students have gone from having a local collection of 40,000 resources to a digital collection of over 200,000 academic e-books and over 1 million Kindle e-books."

The Challenges of All-Digital

Operating in a purely digital environment comes with its own unique set of challenges. Authentication issues that are commonly addressed by librarians and IT [information technology] departments are exacerbated and become even more onerous when libraries provide remote access to their resources.

"The more resources you add to your lineup, the more challenging it becomes," said Corbett. Fisher-Watkins Library uses a single sign-on (SSO) system that allows a user to log in once and gain access to all of the facility's systems without having to repeat the process.

Two years after their traditional library was digitized and reconstructed, Cushing Academy students are using the space very differently.

The SSO system isn't a cure-all for the library's authentication needs. When students use federated search [information retrieval technology that allows the simultaneous search of multiple searchable resources], for example, "delivering those results when students are located off campus can be pretty tricky," said Corbett, whose team is still looking at ways to address that ongoing issue.

Corbett said the library has also run into an issue when attempting to provide access to all digital titles on all mobile devices.

"Because of current [copyright] management, our EBL books don't work with the Kindles," said Corbett, "but they do operate on devices like the Sony e-book and the Nook." He said a Web browser on a laptop can often fill that gap since students don't always read materials cover-to-cover. "In many cases they are just grabbing parts of the content," said Corbett, "so browser access is adequate, but it's still not the distraction-free environment that a paper-based book provides."

Corbett said he hopes that time will resolve some of the challenges he's grappling with. "Part of it is waiting for the technology and the service to get their act together," he said, "and the rest of it is getting the right formats into the students' hands regardless of whether they're using a Kindle, a tablet, or a laptop."

Two years after their traditional library was digitized and reconstructed, Cushing Academy students are using the space very differently than they did in early 2009. They push tables together to work in groups; they check out Kindles and Sony Readers instead of paper books; and they learn about information literacy in one of the building's two classrooms. "It's become a much more open and collaborative space," said Corbett, "instead of just a place where users come to check out materials."

15

United Kingdom Schools Struggle with the Proper Role of Technology

Jessica Shepherd

Jessica Shepherd is an education journalist for The Guardian, *one of the United Kingdom's major daily newspapers.*

School leaders in the United Kingdom (UK) are at odds with technology experts about the use of smartphones and other hand-held computers in the country's classrooms. Many fear UK children are falling behind their foreign counterparts because they lack these high-tech tools. The government is also perceived as contributing to the problem by not possessing a cohesive plan of action to promote the effective use of technology in schools. While the adults argue over strategy, UK students are increasingly purchasing and using smartphones in their personal lives—embracing the latest devices despite the controversy.

Children's learning could "hugely improve" if all pupils were given smartphones to use in the classroom, technology experts say but, instead, the UK [United Kingdom] risks falling behind because "the government doesn't seem that interested in it".

Research shows that in many areas, the majority of pupils own a smartphone, but many schools ban the devices and the National Association of Head Teachers says they hold "potential for mischief and distraction".

Earlier this year, a secondary school in Kent became the first in the country to equip each of its 1,400 pupils with an Apple iPad tablet computer. Longfield academy near Dartford said the iPads would help pupils' learning. Honywood community school in Coggeshall, near Colchester in Essex, has also invested in 1,200 iPads for its pupils. Some schools, such as the Oldershaw academy in Wallasey on Merseyside, have created their own app so parents can check, via their mobiles, what homework their children have been set.

Miles Berry, a senior lecturer in the use of technology in education at the University of Roehampton, said schools needed to "capture the vast amount of informal learning going on outside the classroom".

"The ability to access all the world's information from a handheld device is transformative for learning and would make a huge difference to children's learning from late primary school onwards," he said.

Experts fear the UK will fall behind competitors, such as India and France, unless children have access to a smartphone or similar device.

"It seems wrong to deny this to children inside the classroom when so many already have this opportunity outside the classroom."

Smartphones—mobile phones that offer Internet access and apps—have been proven to help children maximise their learning from the age of nine, education experts say.

Berry said there was "huge enthusiasm" from pupils for using smartphones, but some schools still felt that they needed to be in control of children's learning and that the use of these devices would prevent this.

Other experts fear the UK will fall behind competitors, such as India and France, unless children have access to a smartphone or similar device. But they acknowledge that schools need guidance to ensure their use does not lead to pupils misbehaving, for example by taking photos in lessons.

Recently, Michael Gove, the education secretary, acknowledged that the rate of technological change in education was "rapidly accelerating".

In a speech to the qualifications regulator Ofqual, he said technology had the power to "transform the accuracy and authority" of assessment. "It also gives us the potential to generate yet more data, in order to know how our schools, how our teachers and how our whole system is performing," he said.

Experts predict that within five years, all pupils will be learning on handheld devices.

The government has yet to announce its strategy for information and communications technology (ICT) in schools. A recent event hosted by the rightwing thinktank Policy Exchange concluded that the fact that technology had not "featured prominently" in ministers' speeches has "fuelled fears in some quarters of a lack of clear policy direction in this area".

The government disbanded Becta, the body responsible for promoting technology in schools, almost as soon as it came to power. According to Becta, between 1997 and 2007, Labour spent more than £5bn [billion] on school technology.

Experts predict that within five years, all pupils will be learning on handheld devices. In some parts of California, the handheld devices have already replaced printed textbooks.

Ray Barker, director of the British Educational Suppliers Association, said the technology many pupils carried around with them was often more powerful than the equipment owned by their schools. He urged schools to lift their ban on smartphones.

Valerie Thompson, chief executive of the e-Learning Foundation, a charity that aims to equip disadvantaged children with technology at home and school, said the UK was falling behind, partly because the government had not yet shown clear direction on how it wanted schools to use technology.

"We have been a leader in the deployment of technology in education, but this is changing," she said. "The government doesn't seem that interested in it."

[A 2008 study by Becta] found smartphones helped students to consolidate and reflect on what they had learnt outside lessons.

Thompson suggested schools should buy computers, including smartphones, for their poorest pupils, using money from the "pupil premium"—a government grant for children eligible for free school meals or who have been in care for more than six months. Parents who can afford to, should buy smartphones for their children, she said.

The National Association of Advisors for Computers in Education, which includes teachers, technologists and policymakers, said that in many schools, the majority of pupils owned a smartphone. It cites research that shows the devices can have a "high impact" on students' learning.

Another study, carried out in 2008 by Becta, found smartphones helped students to consolidate and reflect on what they had learnt outside lessons.

A separate study, by Futurelab, a charity that develops innovative approaches to learning, showed smartphones can improve group work.

However, Russell Hobby, general secretary of the National Association of Head Teachers, said the kind of learning that could take place on smartphones was "not all that exciting".

"It should remain with individual schools to determine their policy [on whether they ban the device]," he said.

The government said it would be publishing a strategy on the use of technology in schools before Christmas [2011].

The Department for Education said ICT could not be a substitute for good teaching, but ministers were "clear that its effective use can help raise standards".

"The scale of digital technology in education is developing very rapidly, so we are developing our future approach working closely with industry, school leaders, professional bodies and other experts. ICT is well established in the education sector so we're not going to micro-manage how schools use technology day-to-day."

Organizations to Contact

The editors have compiled the following list of organizations concerned with the issues debated in this book. The descriptions are derived from materials provided by the organizations. All have publications or information available for interested readers. The list was compiled on the date of publication of the present volume; names, addresses, phone and fax numbers, and e-mail and Internet addresses may change. Be aware that many organizations take several weeks or longer to respond to inquiries, so allow as much time as possible.

EducationNext
Harvard Kennedy School, Cambridge, MA   02138
(877) 476-5354 • fax: (617) 496-1507
e-mail: Education_Next@hks.harvard.edu
website: http://educationnext.org

EducationNext is a journal of opinion and research about educational policy. It encourages the open exchange of ideas and gives voice to worthy research and responsible arguments. Its Spring 2012 issue includes an article entitled, "For Digital Learning, the Devil"s in the Details,' which discusses the challenges states are facing in funding and implementing digital learning.

George Lucas Educational Foundation
PO Box 3494, San Rafael, CA   94912-3494
e-mail: info@edutopia.org
website: www.edutopia.org

Edutopia is the educational media resource developed by the George Lucas Educational Foundation. The foundation is dedicated to improving the K-12 learning process by using digital media to document, disseminate, and advocate for innovative, replicable strategies that prepare students to thrive in their future education, careers, and adult lives. Its Edutopia website offers extensive coverage of technology integration in the curriculum.

Hechinger Report

475 Riverside Dr., Suite 650, New York, NY   10115
(212) 870-1072 • fax: (212) 870-1074
e-mail: hechinger@tc.columbia.edu
website: www.hechingerreport.org

The Hechinger Report is a nonprofit news organization that is focused on producing in-depth education journalism. Fewer and fewer reporters at the nation's largest newspapers and wire services are covering national education issues full time. As a result, critical issues do not get the attention they deserve. The organization is trying to fill that gap with analysis and opinion, including insightful stories on how technology is used in education.

International Association for K-12
Online Learning (iNACOL)

1934 Old Gallows Rd., Suite 350, Vienna, VA   22182-4040
(703) 752-6216 • fax: (703) 752-6201
website: www.inacol.org

iNACOL is a nonprofit organization that facilitates collaboration, advocacy, and research to enhance quality K-12 online teaching and learning. iNACOL strives to ensure all students have access to a world-class education and quality online learning opportunities that prepare them for a lifetime of success. Its research on online learning provides analysis of the most promising practices available today.

International Society for Technology in Education (ISTE)

180 W 8th Ave., Suite 300, Eugene, OR   97401-2916
(800) 336-5191 • fax: (541) 302-3778
e-mail: iste@iste.org
website: www.iste.org

ISTE is an association for educators and education leaders that advances excellence in learning and teaching through innovative and effective uses of technology. Its website includes an array of books, journals, and reports that are a practical resource for suggestions on integrating technology in education.

National Center for Technology Innovation (NCTI)
1000 Thomas Jefferson St. NW, Washington, DC   20007
(202) 403-5323 • fax: (202) 403-5001
e-mail: ncti@air.org
website: www.nationaltechcenter.org

NCTI advances learning opportunities for individuals with disabilities by fostering technology innovation. The center assists researchers, product developers, manufacturers, and publishers to create and commercialize products of value to students with special needs. NCTI and the Assistive Technology Industry Association teamed up to create the *Assistive Technology Research Primer,* which includes information for researchers and librarians, along with case studies and experimental results.

New Tech Network
935 Clinton St., Napa, CA   94559
(707) 253-6951 • fax: (707) 253-6993
e-mail: inquiry@newtechnetwork.org
website: www.newtechnetwork.org

New Tech Network operates nationwide with schools, districts, and communities to develop innovative public high schools. The New Tech model provides an instructional approach centered on project-based learning, a culture that empowers students and teachers, and integrated technology in the classroom. It offers numerous examples of schools who are successfully utilizing the New Tech model nationwide.

Office of Educational Technology (OET)
400 Maryland Ave. SW, Washington, DC   20202
(800) 872-5327
website: www.ed.gov/technology

The Office of Educational Technology, in the Office of the Secretary of Education, provides leadership for transforming education through the power of technology. OET develops national educational technology policy and advocates for the transition from print-based to digital learning. The OET provides national surveys, policy research, program evaluations, and the National Education Technology Plan—all tools to guide schools in the planning and implementation of technology.

Partnership for 21st Century Skills (P21)
1 Massachusetts Ave., Suite 700, Washington, DC   20001
(202) 312-6429
e-mail: tvarshavsky@p21.org
website: www.p21.org

P21 is a national organization that advocates for twenty-first century readiness for every student. As the United States continues to compete in a global economy that demands innovation, P21 and its members provide tools and resources to help the US education system keep up by fusing the 3Rs and 4Cs (critical thinking and problem solving, communication, collaboration, and creativity and innovation). The P21 website provides a document detailing its vision for student success in the new global economy entitled: "Framework for 21st Century Learning."

Bibliography

Books

Curtis J. Bonk — *The World Is Open: How World Technology Is Revolutionizing Education.* San Francisco: Jossey-Bass, 2011.

Nicholas Carr — *The Shallows: What the Internet Is Doing to Our Brains.* New York: W.W. Norton and Company, 2010.

Clayton Christensen, Curtis W. Johnson, and Michael B. Horn — *Disrupting Class: How Disruptive Innovation Will Change the Way the World Learns.* New York: McGraw-Hill, 2008.

Tracy Gray and Heidi Silver-Pacuilla — *Breakthrough Technology and Learning: How Educational and Assistive Technologies Are Driving Innovation.* New York: Springer, 2011.

Anya Kamenetz — *DIY U: Edupunks, Edupreneurs, and the Coming Transformation of Higher Education.* White River Junction, VT: Chelsea Green Publishing, 2010.

John Medina — *Brain Rules: 12 Principles for Surviving and Thriving at Work, Home and School.* Seattle, WA: Pear Press, 2009.

John Naisbitt — *Mindset!: Reset Your Thinking and See the Future.* New York: HarperBusiness, 2006.

Don Tapscott   *Grown Up Digital: How the Net Generation Is Changing Your World.* New York: McGraw-Hill, 2008.

Bernie Trilling and Charles Fadel   *21st Century Skills: Learning for Life in Our Times.* San Francisco: Jossey-Bass, 2009.

Tom Vander Ark   *Getting Smart: How Digital Learning Is Changing the World.* San Francisco: Jossey-Bass, 2011.

Periodicals and Internet Sources

Meryl Ain   "Are Schools Getting Too Carried Away With Technology?" Your Education Doctor, October 25, 2011. http://youreducationdoctor.wordpress.com.

Tina Barseghian   "Khan Academy: Out of the Screen, Into the Physical World," MindShift, November 17, 2011. http://blogs.kqed.org/mindshift.

Nicholas Carr   "The Web Shatters Focus, Rewires Brains," *Wired*, May 24, 2011.

Economist   "Flipping the Classroom," September 17, 2011.

Jason Falls   "Social Media Belongs in the Classroom," Education Nation, December 8, 2011. www.educationnation.com.

Lee Fang   "How Online Learning Companies Bought American Schools," *The Nation*, November 16, 2011.

Leigh Goessl — "Op Ed: US Schools Use Varying Philosophies With Computers in Classrooms," *Digital Journal*, December 2, 2011. www.digital journal.com.

Mary Beth Hertz — "A New Understanding of the Digital Divide," Edutopia.com, October 21, 2011.

Joanne Jacobs — "A Technology-free School in Silicon Valley," JoanneJacobs.com, October 27, 2011.

Autumn Kelley — "Involve, Prepare, Apply, and Develop: iPads in the Classroom," *Tech and Learning*, March 23, 2011.

Eric Lawson — "iPads, iPod Touches, and iPhones as Assistive Technology in Education," *Tech and Learning*, March 28, 2011.

Cheryl Lemke and Ed Coughlin — "The Change Agents," *Educational Leadership*, September 2009.

Aran Levasseur — "The Pedagogy of Play and the Role of Technology in Learning," MediaShift, January 3, 2012. www.pbs.org/mediashift.

Arthur E. Levine — "The School of One: The School of Tomorrow," *Huffington Post*, September 16, 2009. www .huffingtonpost.com.

Harold Levy — "Educated Nation?" *Hechinger Report*, September 28, 2011. www.hechinger report.org.

Zara McAlister   "Social Network Squag Aims to Be a Safe Place for Autistic Kids," *Financial Post*, February 8, 2012. http://business.financialpost.com.

Bridget McCrea   "Creating an Ultra-Flexible Learning Space," *THE Journal*, February 8, 2012. www.thejournal.com.

Heidi Mitchell   "Two Families, Two Takes on Virtual Schooling," *Wall Street Journal*, December 15, 2011.

Paul Takahashi   "Schools Seeing Improvement in Math Scores as Students Play Video Games," *Las Vegas Sun*, February 8, 2012.

Greg Toppo   "eCheating: Students Find High Tech Ways to Deceive Teachers," *USA Today*, December 16, 2011.

Alex Wilhelm   "How Technology Has Changed Education," TNW: The Next Web, January 5, 2011. www.thenextweb .com.

Index

CPSIA information can be obtained
at www.ICGtesting.com
Printed in the USA
FFOW041356280213
933FF